GET MARRIED, STAY MARRIED

PAUL AND BILLIE TSIKA

GET MARRIED, STAY MARRIED

DESTINY IMAGE® PUBLISHERS, INC.

P.O. Box 310, Shippensburg, PA 17257-0310

"Speaking to the Purposes of God for This Generation and for the Generations to Come."

This book and all other Destiny Image, Revival Press, MercyPlace, Fresh Bread, Destiny Image Fiction, and Treasure House books are available at Christian bookstores and distributors worldwide.

For a U.S. bookstore nearest you, call 1-800-722-6774.

For more information on foreign distributors, call 717-532-3040.

Reach us on the Internet: www.destinyimage.com.

Trade Paper ISBN: 978-0-7684-3273-2
Hardcover ISBN: 978-0-7684-3501-6
Large Print ISBN: 978-0-7684-3502-3
Ebook ISBN: 978-0-7684-9092-3

For Worldwide Distribution, Printed in the U.S.A.

1 2 3 4 5 6 7 8 9 10 11 / 15 14 13 11 10

DEDICATION

This book is dedicated in loving memory to my dad and mom, Carl Edward Rexroad and Opal Elizabeth Hodges Rexroad. They were married May 21, 1942, in Houma, Louisiana. If it weren't for them, there would be no me! They both had very hard lives growing up, so they never learned how to verbally express their love. However, they showed their love for their children in so many ways. I praise God for the parents he chose for me.

I also want to thank God for Angelo Demetri Tsika and Kathryn Marie Jamison Tsika. They were my in-laws from the time I was 19 until their deaths. They loved me like a daughter and were a refuge for me during the first four turbulent years of my married life in Sanford, Maine. I loved them dearly. They gave me the greatest gift I have on earth, my husband, Paul.

❧

I dedicate my part of this book in loving memory to Angelo and Kathryn Tsika, my parents. I remember always being provided for by my parents. I believe they did the best they could with what they knew. We saw the struggles and heard the arguments but always believed they would stay together. This alone brought great security to all five children. They were married December 21, 1939, in Millinocket, Maine. They lived in a day when couples made their marriage work, and they did. My greatest regret is that I never loved them as I should have. I miss them.

I also want to thank God for Carl and Opal, Billie's parents. When Carl passed and Opal came to live with us, I began for the first time to appreciate how hard life must have been for them. If not for them, I would not have my wife, Billie Kaye, who is as my own soul. She is the joy of my life on earth. I cannot imagine life without her.

Both of our parents got married and stayed married to each other until they passed. They left us a great legacy of commitment to the marriage covenant in spite of all the challenges life brought their way.

Thank you Carl and Opal, Angelo and Kathryn.

Paul and Billie

ACKNOWLEDGMENTS

We first of all want to acknowledge our wonderful Lord Jesus who has given grace for every mile and strength for every trial. All wisdom and insight comes from Him and all the glory goes to Him.

Destiny Image Publishers. For their insights, knowledge, and patience in knowing how to bring a book to life.

Rick and Melissa Killian. For taking a ton of material, scattered and sometimes vague thoughts, and making us look good.

World Wide Dream Builders. They have allowed us a platform on which to learn more about relationships than we ever dreamed possible.

David Hyman. My dear friend who initially gave me the shove needed to write a book on marriage. His reasoning was that between Billie and me with our children, we have over 100 years of marriage experience to share.

ENDORSEMENTS

Get Married, Stay Married is a book written by a couple who have lived their message for many years. I have watched my friends Paul and Billie Tsika model the principles they write about and it works! Buy this book only if you want practical, relevant, and biblical insight into your marriage relationship.

John C. Maxwell
Author and Speaker

Georgia Lee and I are very excited for you to have Paul and Billie Kaye Tsika's new book as a resource for your marriage. We have been dear friends for many years and have worked closely together. We have seen firsthand the results of their ministry both in their own family and our organization. True success to us is meaningless unless it begins at home. Nobody understands how to negotiate the thin line between marital success and business success better than Paul and Billie. Our prayer is that you will believe and apply the principles of *Get Married, Stay Married* for a truly successful life.

Ron and Georgia Lee Puryear
President, World Wide Dream Builders
www.wwdb.com

Investing wisely in our marriages reaps huge rewards in every area of our lives. When it comes to marriage, there is no better team than Paul and Billie Kaye Tsika. This book has been an important study for my wife and me, and now it is the most important gift we give to couples we love.

Rick Green
Speaker, Author, and Host of
"WallBuilders Live! with David Barton"

If a virus has attacked your marriage and you are about to hit the delete button of divorce, it would behoove you to spend a little time reading this amazing account of how two people can overcome even the most seemingly insurmountable marriage obstacles. As an eyewitness to this healing miracle of God, I can attest to the accounts of God's mighty intervention and how He brought the Tsika's through. What the Holy Spirit did for them, He can do for you.

Pastor Mike Whitson
First Baptist Church
Indian Trail, North Carolina

Contents

FOREWORD

Be assured of this: Paul and Billie Tsika are the real deal! You can take to the bank as truth what they say. What they say has arisen from what they are—real all the time with everyone and especially each other. It is wonderful when you can see through people to the real person when the real person is who you have been observing all along. To know Paul and Billie is to love them—to know them thoroughly, to love them deeply. I am not only recommending that wise people read what they have written...anything they have written. What they say about their marriage is not merely rhetoric or theory but the tried and true experience of weathering the storm that few marriages have survived. You and your spouse will profit from their experience whether you have been married half a year or half a century.

Good going, Paul and Billie!

Jack Taylor, President
Dimensions Ministries
Melbourne, Florida

INTRODUCTION

In a time when nothing is more certain than change, the commitment of two people to one another has become difficult and rare. Yet, by its scarcity, the beauty and value of this exchange have only been enhanced. —Robert Sexton

*M*y wife, Billie, and I have been especially grieved in recent years as we've watched an increasing number of marriages crumble before our very eyes. Dear friends we have known for years have made choices totally inconsistent with what we believed their values to be. Did our friends deceive us, or have our friends been deceived?

The question we have so often asked ourselves while shaking our heads: "Have these friends become so hardened, so blinded, so indifferent to those they love that they are able to abandon spouse, children, and a marriage they had committed to honor for a lifetime?" How do they become so convinced that the consequences of their life-altering choices will be "the best for everyone"—that their decisions to divorce won't devastate children, negatively affect communities, and create a heritage of rejection for generations to come?

As marriage counselors, we have seen firsthand the carnage left in the wake of divorce. We've seen the damaged children and dejected spouses caused by the discarded promises of being together "for better or for worse." We have counseled people in second marriages still reeling from the effects of the end of their first. We have seen young couples starting out so in love they thought they would float into eternity together on clouds of marital bliss only to return months later wondering how they had ever been crazy enough to marry each other.

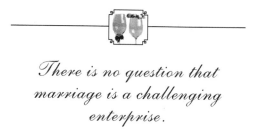

There is no question that marriage is a challenging enterprise.

There is no question that marriage is a challenging enterprise. It is not for the faint of heart. But while we have seen marriages fail, we know they can succeed. In the 44 years Billie Kaye and I have been married, we have learned a great deal about the ups and downs of marriage, but more importantly, we have learned a great deal about how to turn the "for worse" times into a "for better" future. As a result, our three children have strong marriages that have lasted 23, 22, and 19 years respectively. We've used the wisdom we have learned—or perhaps it is better to say "earned"—to help them overcome different challenges and struggles.

We have also shared the same wisdom with the hundreds of other couples we have counseled and have watched as it bore fruit in their families and marriages. In all of that time, we have learned a simple truth—in marriage, *the heart of the problem is the problem of the heart.* In other words, when you can deal honestly and openly with the issues of your own heart, there are virtually no obstacles you can't overcome in your marriage.

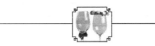

In marriage, the heart of the problem is the problem of the heart.

Jeremiah says in Lamentations 3:42, *"We have transgressed and rebelled."* Transgression is crossing over the line, but rebellion is a refusal to step back over it again. In marriage, we make mistakes and we hurt each other, but making marriage successful means first being brutally honest with ourselves and dealing with our own heart issues—only then will we find our way back over the line to a truly loving relationship again.

As I write this book, I thank God for helping me get back over that line when I found I had transgressed. I have learned how painful it is to find yourself on the other side and what it takes to cross back over again once and for all. It is our sincerest desire to help struggling couples not even *get near* that line—and for anyone who has crossed it, to help them return to the sanity, safety, and sanctity of their marriages on the right side together reconciled and renewed.

Successful marriages require honest, open, transparent, and even courageous communication.

Successful marriages are always a growth process that require honest, open, transparent, and even courageous communication. If you are willing to walk with us through the pages of this book, then we can help you learn some of the secrets to keeping your marriage alive and joyful. We implore every reader to look deep into the mirror of his or her own life and marriage and see what it is telling them about who they are. Use all of the failures and hindsight offered in these chapters as your foresight for a great future. Learn to treasure your spouse and children and they will bless you with a lifetime of wonderful memories that will follow you into eternity.

CHAPTER 1

YOUR MARRIAGE IS NOT AN ACCIDENT

Happy marriages begin when we marry the ones we love, and they blossom when we love the ones we marry. —Tom Mullen

Whenever I think about my 44 years with Billie, our marriage, and how God brought us together, I'm amazed at the grace God has given us to persevere. God is sovereign and in charge of our lives. We can trust Him to direct us to where we need to go to fulfill His purpose for our lives—as well as draw us into the lifetime relationship that will complete the good work He has begun in us. God designed your spouse to complete you—to strengthen, temper, embolden, refine, and perfect you—and to facilitate His plans and purposes concerning you. God designed marriage to be a blessing, but also as a means of helping you grow into everything He created you to be.

"For I know the plans I have for you," declares the Lord, "plans to prosper you and not to harm you, plans to give you hope and a future" (Jeremiah 29:11 NIV).

I am so grateful that God brought Billie Kaye into my life. I am certain that God engineered her with the necessary strength, grace, patience, determination, and courage to be married to the likes of me. When I think of God's will concerning my marriage to Billie Kaye, I think of what the Lord told Jeremiah, *"For I know the plans I have for you...plans to prosper you and not to harm you, plans to give you hope and a future"* (Jer. 29:11 NIV). It might not seem like that today concerning you and your marriage, but whatever trials you are going through with your spouse, they are aligned with God's plans to perfect and prosper you—to maximize your greatest potential—to give you a rich present and a rewarding future.

However, I am also a realist. I know your marriage today might not be all you had hoped it would be the day you recited your vows to one another. Billie and I have counseled enough couples to know the heartaches that can result from trusting your hopes, aspirations, and heart to another and feeling that person is not being faithful with that trust. We know how marriage can seemingly make a devil out of the very angel you thought you had married.

Love and marriage can be funny things. Sometimes the very same traits we thought were so endearing and wonderful about our spouse when we "fell in love" are what drive us crazy about them years later. It is commonly said that "opposites attract"—but what happens when all of those little opposites turn into big irritants? Looking back on why you married your husband or wife, maybe you'll be able to identify with some of these "before" and "after" scenarios.

Husband to Wife:

Before: *She takes my breath away!*
After: *I feel like I'm suffocating!*

Wife to Husband:

Before: *I love the way he takes charge of a situation.*
After: *He is a controlling, manipulative, dominating psycho!*

Husband to Wife:

Before: *I love her unique sense of fashion.*
After: *Is she really going to wear that in public?*

Wife to Husband:

Before: *It's so nice how he eats everything I put in front of him.*
After: *Is he really going to eat all that?*

Husband to Wife:

Before: *I love how I'm always the center of her attention.*
After: *I just need some space!*

Although these are funny to read, changing perceptions and attitudes can cause seemingly insurmountable stress and frustration. I'm sure you've heard the old saying, "While the husband hopes his wife will never change, the wife dreams of nothing but changing her husband." Our dreams of marital bliss can easily turn into nightmares beyond the honeymoon. What is important to remember is that these types of challenges are common to every marriage. The fact is that as long as there are differences between men and women, there will be differences to overcome in our marriages!

I understand these challenges can easily become overwhelming, and the hurts that result can seem irreparable. Yet too often people end up divorced and are left as disoriented and broken in spirit as the victim of a hit and run driver. That was never part of God's plan for you.

Yes, there are situations where divorce, for the safety and sanity of one or both partners, is justified and the only way forward. In situations of abuse and unrepentant, repeated infidelity or abandonment, for example, the marriage has been broken even before the word "divorce" is ever mentioned. But God never intends for marriages to come to that. He is the God of second (and third and fourth!) chances. If you will let Him, He will work with you to repair everything that has been broken, reconcile the most divisive conflicts, and resolve even the most challenging circumstances.

Whatever ordeals you are going through with your spouse, they are not outside of God's influence and aid.

I want you to know that whatever ordeals you are going through with your spouse, they are not outside of God's influence and aid. It may feel like someone is taking a knife to your heart, but if you will work it through with your spouse, you will see it is divine surgery that will allow you to be freer and more in love than you have ever been.

You marrying who you did was no accident. The crazy series of events that brought you to your spouse—whether a long and circuitous journey or a brief one—were orchestrated by God as part of His plan for your life. Because of that, He has a vested interest in seeing you succeed. No matter what you're going through or how dark it seems, the Master Counselor is always present with the light you need to take the next step toward a great marriage.

What God Has Joined Together

I remember the first day I saw Billie Kaye. It was in February 1966. I was reporting for duty to Master Gunnery Sergeant Taylor at the Parris Island Marine Corps base in South Carolina. We were both in the service. As I walked through the doors of headquarters and headed up the stairs to Sergeant Taylor's office, I saw Billie coming down. I fell in love with her at that very moment. I'll never forget how my mind raced thinking about how I could get to know this beautiful woman.

I felt like she was probably the kind of gal who never stuck with any guy for very long. She was too pretty for that. I was sure she was never without someone asking her out, especially in the middle of a boot camp full of Marines. I don't know if she believes me to this day, but because I wanted to get her attention, when she said "Hi," I turned and looked the other way. It seemed to have worked. She was intrigued enough to ask around about me, and it wasn't long before I made sure I was the only guy she paid attention to again.

A short time later, we met face to face at the Non-Commissioned Officers' (NCO) Club on base. Six weeks later, on April 28, we were married. I look back on it now and think, "What a miracle!" How could I ever doubt that God directed our circumstances toward each other from the very beginning, even though we didn't know Him at the time.

Despite God's plan, our first few years together were very difficult.

Despite God's plan, our first few years together were very difficult. Neither one of us knew how to treat the other, nor were we part of any church or organization that could advise us about how to make marriage work. We were young and immature and knew nothing about love beyond the intense emotion we felt toward each other. The one thing I did know was that I loved Billie Kaye. Many would say there is no such thing as love at first sight, but Billie captured my heart the moment I laid eyes on her. I will not deny that I was attracted to her physically—she was and is still so very beautiful—but something far deeper was happening in my heart at the same time.

I am reminded of when Abraham sent his servant to find a bride for his son Isaac in chapter 24 of Genesis. The servant found Rebekah at a well and returned with her to his master. When she saw Isaac coming toward them, *"Rebekah lifted her eyes, and when she saw Isaac she dismounted from her camel."* Then she asked, *"Who is this man walking in the field to meet us?"* and the servant replied, *"It is my master."* The passage goes on to state that Isaac *"took Rebekah and she became his wife, and he loved her."*

The story doesn't give an account of what was going through Isaac's mind as he saw Rebekah approaching, or how Rebekah felt as she spotted Isaac, but I imagine they both experienced a deep sense of destiny—and that is what happened to me when I first saw Billie Kaye. It may have taken Billie a little longer, but eventually she came around to the same realization.

The Other Side of the Story

When I saw Paul that day in 1966, I had just returned from my first leave after being assigned to Parris Island. I had only joined the Marine Corps six months earlier, which was only 11 days after I had graduated from high school. I remember our first meeting as if it were yesterday. I was walking down the stairs when the "new driver" came walking up. What struck me first were his beautiful green eyes. I also remember seeing the name on his uniform and not being able to pronounce it. As I was walking down the stairs I said, "Hi," but he looked the other way as if he hadn't heard me. The next time I saw him was a few days later "holding up a wall" at the NCO Club. He was drunk as a skunk. Believe it or not, I think that was the moment I fell in love with him.

How I fell for a man who was drunk I will never know. I had a profound aversion to men who drank because my dad had been a drunkard for the first ten years of his and my mom's marriage. I was painfully aware of how my mother suffered because of his drinking. I remember standing outside beer joints with my siblings while mom wept as we waited for my dad to come out. I would not have chosen to fall in love with someone who abused alcohol, but there I was falling for this man in a drunken stupor!

From that night on, I bugged my friends to help me find a way to date him. Then one night, we all went to the beach, built a bonfire, and Paul and I ended up talking until morning. We were together every night after that. We were both afraid to tell the other we were falling in love, but once we did, we immediately started talking about marriage. Paul's tour of duty would be up in six months, and I wanted to be with him when he began the next phase of his life. The only possible way for me to be discharged at the same time would be if I were pregnant. It seemed getting married as soon as possible was the reasonable thing to do.

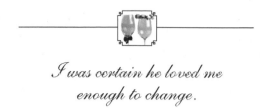

*I was certain he loved me
enough to change.*

We planned to get married during the next 96-hour pass we could arrange. We set the date for April 28. Paul had stopped drinking the last two weeks we were dating and I foolishly figured that meant he would never drink again. We had only known each other a month and a half before we got married, and as young and naive as I was, I thought those two sober weeks were enough to prove he was the man of my dreams. After all, I thought, we were going to be husband and wife and start a family; I was certain he loved me enough to change. I never doubted his intentions or his integrity.

Yet the night before the ceremony, his friends threw him a bachelor party, and he drank as if he had never stopped. Then, in a sudden angry rage, he flew off the handle and started yelling at me. That was the end of the party and his friends left. We went out and sat in the car to cool off, but he was still mad. He tried to throw our wedding rings out of the window, but somehow I put up my hand and blocked them so they fell to the floor instead. Nine hours later, we were married. You should see our wedding picture—I looked like a scared rabbit!

Paul had a volatile temper that intensified when he drank. Not only that, he had a long history of disruptive behavior as a Marine. He had gotten into numerous violent fights and had been busted down in rank four different times. It was due to his wild behavior that he was sent back to Parris Island as a driver to finish out his last six months of duty. Apparently they didn't know what else to do to keep him out of trouble.

God used what seemed to be a series of unrelated events to direct Paul and me to what would become the path we are on today.

Looking back, God was at work all of the time bringing us together. He used what seemed to be a series of unrelated events to direct him and me to what would become the path we are on today. Who would have thought that God would use an unruly, undisciplined, drunken Marine to someday counsel married couples and coach business leaders? Who would have imagined that God would use our marriage that started in such a surprising way to bring healing and restoration to hundreds of couples across the nation?

Falling in Love Is Not Enough

There is no question that Billie Kaye and I fell hard for each other, and that falling in love was an overwhelming thing for us. It is certainly not the way we would counsel young couples getting married today! For a while, that "falling in love" euphoria covered up our differences and irritations, but that didn't last very long. It is as easy to "fall out" of that kind of love as it is to "fall into" it. True love, on the other hand, is not about that overwhelming emotion that can blind you—it is something more. It is something that builds a bond between the two of you despite your differences that even overshadows how you "feel."

Billie and I came from totally different backgrounds. I was raised in northern Maine, and she was raised in southern Texas. I was morally bad; she was morally good. I was out of church; she was in church. I was raised Roman Catholic; she was raised a Baptist. We were from opposite sides of the world in every way.

At the time we met, I was coming back from overseas with only six months left in my Marine Corps service; she had just finished basic training. They just happened to station me at Parris Island where Billie Kaye just happen to be stationed. I just happened to be assigned as a driver at recruit classification where Billie just happeneded to be working. We just happened to meet, happened to fall in love, and happened to marry—but the fact that we have now been married for 44 years didn't just happen. That took some decisive steps on both of our parts.

Trials and challenges are what make love grow stronger—if you commit to working through them.

We don't know of any strong marriage that hasn't had some rough or rocky times in the first few years, and that was certainly our experience as well. Marriage is not for the faint of heart! Enduring love is tried and tested by difficult personalities, debilitating setbacks, and sometimes devastating circumstances. Trials and challenges are what make love grow stronger if we commit to working through them.

As much as we want to simply "fall into love" as if it were a hot bath and "live happily ever after" as if never having to get out of it again, that is not how real love works. There is no mindlessly falling into a lasting love. It takes dogged determination to make it work. Love is not something that overtakes you as much as something you overtake.

There are three reasons "falling in love" isn't enough to build a life together:

1. Falling in love is not an act of the will or a conscious choice, therefore we have no control over it. No matter how much we may want to fall in love, we cannot make it happen. We may not even be seeking the experience when it overtakes us. As a result, people tend to fall in love at inopportune times and with unlikely people.

2. Falling in love is not real love because it is effortless. Whatever we do in the "in love" state requires little discipline or conscious effort on our part, therefore there is little we can do to make it last.

3. Falling in love does not consider the growth of the

other. In the fog of falling in love, you don't care that the other person needs to grow as much as you want to maintain how being with them makes you feel.[1]

On the other hand, true love—the love that is necessary to make marriage work after "falling in love" wears off—is a conscious act of the will requiring great effort and is primarily concerned with the growth of, or what is best for, the other. This kind of love is intentional, divinely ordained, and requires a supernatural grace to overcome your own weaknesses, past hurts, and selfish desires. It is not an easy love to show to your spouse, but it is the only truly rewarding one. It is the only love that has the potential to make the honeymoon last a lifetime.

The Early Years

It seems it was less than a month after Paul and I got married that I became pregnant, even though it wouldn't be until August that Paul would be discharged. As the end of the summer approached, I was nearly bursting out of my uniform, yet the red tape wouldn't allow me to leave the service. Thankfully my supervisor, the master gunnery sergeant, was an incredibly kind man who told me to stay home and take care of myself.

When August came, everything was finally in place for us to leave together, so we made a trip to Texas to visit my family before heading back to Maine where Paul was from. I was visibly pregnant with Gretchen by the time Paul met my parents. My dad was a bit of a character who acted like he thought he was Wyatt Earp. When he saw Paul, he said, "Get over here

Yankee! I want to take a look at you!" As I remember him from my childhood, he was always smoking a cigarette and drinking a Dr. Pepper. I think he scared Paul half to death, but once they became better acquainted they got along pretty well.

I was all alone in a strange place with no other friends or family.

When we got to Maine, I fell in love with Paul's parents right away. They took me in as if I were their own daughter. That was a good thing too, because I was all alone in a strange place with no other friends or family. When Paul started drinking again, their home became a place of refuge for Gretchen and me. Back then Paul didn't just drink socially, he drank until he was so stone drunk he was vile and scary. I would quickly get out of the house and take Gretchen to his parent's home until he sobered up.

He seemed to have a lot of things boiling beneath the surface that he was dealing with, and they would come out looking for a fight when he drank. Eventually he had so many DWI (Driving While Intoxicated) offenses, that the state of Maine was threatening to take his license away. That was one of the factors that inspired us to move to Texas in hopes of making a clean start. However, that would not have worked out either had Paul not found something else in Texas that would transform his life.

Discovering True Love

When we got to Texas in 1970, I had made the commitment to Billie that I would stop drinking. It was only a few months later, however, that I ended up in a bar one night drunk enough to get into a violent fight that could easily have landed me in jail. No matter how badly I wanted to change, I couldn't. I didn't know what to do.

Some time later, Billie's parents invited us to go to church with them in Corpus Christi. It wasn't the first time that Billie and I had gone to church together, but it was the first time I had gone and heard the story of Jesus with my heart, not just my ears. There I was looking for a way to change and in that church service I heard it for the first time. I heard there was a way to escape the pain and anger of my life, and it had to do with understanding and accepting the love that comes from God alone.

You would have thought I would be overjoyed about that, but my reaction was to run, literally. I ran out of that auditorium, but what I had heard didn't leave me. I wrestled with it for the next three months. Then when I heard the message again in Victoria, Texas, at the end of that time, I ran again. Somehow I knew it was the change I needed, but it also scared me to the core.

The next day in downtown Victoria, that particular pastor just happened to see me in a typewriter shop on Main Street. He came in and started talking with me. Again, he told me the story of Jesus and how He wanted to forgive me, come into my life, and free me from the mistakes of my past if I would only give my life to Him. Again I ran—out of the shop and down the street—but he followed me and caught up with me on a street corner some distance away. He asked me again, "Why don't you let Jesus come into your heart and life and save you?" I avoided his gaze and made excuses, but he kept on asking me the same question over and over again.

Finally I had no more excuses. I broke down right there knowing I needed Jesus. I knew I needed forgiveness and despite all of my upbringing and past anger, I fell to my knees right there in the gutter in front of my car and asked Jesus into my life. My life truly changed that day. It was so significant I remember the exact date: May 11, 1971.

In an instant, my heart was transformed because of that decision. I would have to make many more tough decisions in the years to come, decisions that would help me grow, but the happiness Billie and I have today started with the decision I made that day on Main Street.

I had promised to turn over a new leaf only to discover it was rotten on both sides.

The point I want to make here is that meeting God on that street corner gave me the power to overcome myself that I had not previously had. When we moved to Texas, I had promised to turn over a new leaf only to discover it was rotten on both sides. I couldn't escape myself. But when I heard that message in Corpus Christi, I realized that the reason I couldn't change was because only God could put inside of me what I needed to become the man I wanted to be. I ran scared for three months, but God caught up with me in Victoria, and I have never been the same. I immediately stopped drinking, and my violent temper ceased for a while. I started attending church, as well as reading the Bible, listening to tapes, and learning as much about God as I could. That change saved our marriage. I found I had a new love in my heart that overcame my selfishness and began to change me in ways I had never thought possible. Though I didn't fully realize it at the time, I began to know real love and see it transform my life and marriage.

I'd like to say things only got better from then on, but the truth is we would have even tougher times to face in the coming years. However, I can say the troubles we had before that time were because I didn't know any better—in some ways I was like a scared, injured animal striking out at anything that moved—while the troubles we would face later were because I didn't choose to exercise what I had come to know as real love.

Endnote

1. M. Scott Peck, M.D., *The Road Less Traveled: A New Psychology of Love, Traditional Values, and Spiritual Growth* (New York: Simon and Schuster, 2002), 88

Chapter 2

What Is True Love?

Marriage is not a noun; it's a verb. It isn't something you get. It's something you do. It's the way you love your partner every day. —Barbara De Angelis

$\mathscr{B}$efore we go any further, I want to talk a bit more about the kind of love I started to learn about that day in Victoria. This book is about making love last a lifetime, and for that to happen, we have to learn what real love truly is and how it works. So what is love *really*? How are we wired to love? How can we know that our love is true and not based on an emotional feeling? How much do our feelings really have to do with it? What about satisfying my own important needs and desires? What about reciprocity?

There is no way that your differences in upbringing and personal habits won't at some time aggravate your spouse, even if you don't have it as bad as we did with my violent temper and drinking. As mentioned previously, even the things that we thought most endearing before marriage can become irritations down the road. We are all different people—sometimes that is good, and sometimes that's a problem. Although the rule is that opposites attract, there is no promise opposites will always get along! That takes something more than just attraction and "falling in love." Even when the differences are fairly minor, you can allow a wedge to be driven between your spouse and yourself if you don't understand the type of love required to overcome them.

The truth is, being married makes us face some feelings and character traits we may never have had to face had we stayed single. We believe God intended marriage to make us holy as much as to make us happy. There will always be a tremendous amount of immaturity within each of us that marriage will cause us to confront. The trouble is that the romantic and sensual view of marriage we get from television and movies has caused us to have unrealistic expectations. Movies are good at portraying the "falling into" but not so good with the "lasting" aspects of love. If the purpose of marriage were simply to live in a state of continual romantic infatuation, we would have to change our spouse every couple of years instead of changing ourselves.

On the other hand, if we really want to see God transform us from the inside out, we will need to concentrate on changing our own hearts rather than trading in our spouse. We may also find that the more difficult our spouse appears to be, the greater the opportunity we have to grow. Keep in mind that it is more of a process of completion than it is alteration. God never designed marriage for us to change each other, but for us to complete each other.

If the purpose of marriage were simply to live in a state of continual romantic infatuation, we would have to change our spouse every couple of years instead of changing ourselves.

Understanding that there are different types of love will help you get a better perspective of the one kind of love you should be focusing on in your marriage, though in a good marriage all three are often present at the same time.

The most commonly *felt* kind of love is romantic, physical, and sensual—it is the "falling in love" kind of love. This kind of love is called *eros*—it is where the word *erotic* comes from and represents the sexual side of love. Essentially, the basis of *eros* is self-seeking—self-satisfying—and sees the other more as an object to be won and conquered than as an individual to be cherished and honored.

In marriage, and only in marriage, however, *eros* can be transformed. Within the commitment of marriage, *eros* can be about sharing sexuality together as husband and wife. In this way, *eros* can bring a special intimacy to marriage, but no marriage is safe if built on it alone. While we may fall in *eros* and get married, we can also fall out of *eros* very easily when times get tough. However, if you choose to make the other types of love consistent parts of your life and your marriage, you will fall in *eros* all over again with your spouse and continue to enjoy that aspect of your marriage for years to come. Only in marriage can *eros* become something that is more about giving to the other than about taking from them. Such romance should continue throughout your lives together.

Essentially, the basis of eros is self-seeking—self-satisfying—and sees the other more as an object to be won and conquered than as an individual to be cherished and honored.

The second kind of love is called *phileo* love, which means "brotherly love," and is the kind of love shared between close friends. It is the base of the word *Philadelphia*, the "city of brotherly love." It is more emotional than it is physical. It is the familiar, comforting love of friends and family. I know of no marriage that has lasted where the husband and wife are not as much best friends as they are lovers. It is not enough for us to love our spouses—we must also like them. We must enjoy one another's company, doing things together, sharing interests, and pursuing common goals.

Where *phileo* falls short is that, although this is more of a mutual love than *eros*, it is also conditional. If you meet my needs, I'll meet your needs. When you stop meeting my needs, I'll stop meeting your needs. The relationship is often easily broken because it can be based more on what two people have in common than a commitment to stick with each other through times of differences and animosity.

The third and final type of love is the very glue that keeps marriages together. It is a selfless, unconditional, supernatural love called *agape*. This is the self-sacrificing love we find exemplified by Jesus—which is why it is also the most challenging for most of us to exercise. We are called by God to employ this kind of love at all times, especially with those to whom we are the closest. This is why it is so important to begin with your spouse. How can we walk in that kind of love with strangers and enemies if we can't even exercise such a love in our own homes?

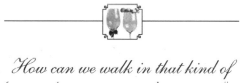

How can we walk in that kind of love with strangers and enemies if we can't even exercise such a love in our own homes?

Learning to walk in *agape* love is so important that the apostle Paul told the Corinthians without it they were nothing (see 1 Cor. 13:2). It doesn't matter if you give away all of your belongings to the poor, if you've taught great wisdom to millions, built an incredible business, moved mountains with your faith, or given your life to be martyred for the innocent—without this kind of love, it all amounts to nothing. Paul went on to describe exactly what this kind of love looks like:

> *Agape is patient and kind. Agape is not jealous or boastful or proud or rude. It does not demand its own way. It is not irritable, and it keeps no record of being wronged. It does not rejoice about injustice but rejoices whenever the truth wins out. Agape never gives up, never loses faith, is always hopeful, and endures through every circumstance* (1 Corinthians 13:4-7 [paraphrased]).

The most valuable thing we've been given is the opportunity to love one another with this kind of love. *Agape* love in this sense is not a noun or an adjective—it is not something you "fall into" or can use to describe what you are "in" or "out" of—it is a verb requiring an active decision of the will to behave in a certain way. It's not about what others do, but entirely about what you do. The burden to love is placed squarely on your shoulders. To love someone in this way is an ongoing decision that requires premeditated intention and conscious action.

*To love someone in this way is
an ongoing decision that requires
premeditated intention and conscious
action.*

Learning to Love With True Love

Agape love is not something you feel, but something you practice whether you feel like it or not. Most of us have to practice being patient and kind and giving until it becomes a habit. You've got to remind yourself daily not to get offended or insist on your own rights. You must constantly remind yourself to resist selfishness, which is not a very natural thing to do. Most of us are governed by our feelings, emotions, or selfish perspectives—none of which encourage us to give others the benefit of the doubt when disputes arise, or lay aside self-interest for the sake of the interests of others.

Have you ever asked yourself how someone could choose to give away everything to feed the poor, or sacrifice their life for the greater good, and not have love? The reason is that there are a lot of people who give that aren't motivated by love as much as self-interest. They want to look good to others. If you give away all of your possessions or even your life in order to get something in return, that does not make it an act of real love—real love, *agape* love, gives without expecting anything in return.

God knows the motives of the heart. Your giving to your spouse cannot be motivated by something you are hoping to get in return. If it is, it is conditional and temporary. Love that is conditional will eventually be disappointed and hurt; love that is unconditional will never be.

With this in mind, ask yourself: "What is the opposite of love?" Is it hate? Is it anger? No. It is selfishness. I find when I'm easily provoked or offended, the reason is that I am not motivated by true love, but selfishly holding onto my own "rights" or sense of how I "deserve" to be treated. When I am impatient or rude—things that are contrary to love—I find I am motivated by my own self-interest.

Selfishness is consumed with getting, while love is preoccupied with giving. That is why I've always said that *the heart of the problem is the problem of the heart.* Hurting or selfish hearts struggle with *agape* love—they need to experience healing, forgiveness, and true *agape* love before they are capable of truly loving unselfishly.

*Selfishness is consumed with getting,
while love is preoccupied with giving.*

Most people we counsel are not ignorant of their own selfishness. They know what the right thing to do is, but they have trouble winning the battle over their own wants, needs, and desires. Oftentimes it is simply a matter of finding the courage and strength and willingness to do what they know is right to do—and then deliberately and continually practicing it. As I have learned, this is impossible to do without a personal relationship with God, for He is the only source of *agape* love. This was the love that I found in that street gutter in Victoria, Texas, that would become the basis for keeping our marriage together for the next 40-some years.

First Comes Love, Then Comes Marriage...

When you're in love, it's hard to believe you will ever see anything other than perfection in your spouse. You are convinced you will make each other supremely happy every single day for the rest of your lives. Perhaps you're not completely naïve. Yes, you know you have some differences, however, you are certain they are nothing you can't handle or are really that important.

You believe that you and your spouse will openly discuss anything that comes up honestly and candidly—that one of you will always be willing to make concessions even in the toughest of disagreements, and you will never go to bed angry. Your relationship is strong, your communication skills are sharp, your commitment is unwavering, and there is nothing the two of you can't face down together. That, my friends, is the intoxication of "falling in love."

The "in love" experience, for better or worse, can be blinding. Perhaps it is God's way of making sure we cement our relationship before we turn tail and run. Once we descend from the clouds, however, and our eyes are opened, we see all of the imperfections and shortcomings of the other and wonder how we could have ever overlooked them before. We grew up thinking we would fall in love, ride off into the sunset, and live happily ever after. We believed our spouse would always be on his or her best behavior, courteous and mannerly, always speaking kindly, always looking their best, never overindulging, always making the best use of their time, and certainly never making unwise financial decisions. Yet, when these shortcomings seemingly pop out of nowhere, we think, "If I had only known!"

Once these waves of reality begin to set in, we might start to second-guess our commitment. Perhaps our first thought is that we should look for a way out of the relationship. Instead, though, most of us will begin to coexist and adopt a pattern of being "around" each other more than being "together." Then slowly over the years we grow apart, and then wanting to avoid discomfort, we separate. We blame it on having "fallen out of love," and we withdraw, separate, divorce, and then set off in search of a new "falling in love" experience.

But that is not what being married is all about—nor is it where the real joy of relationship exists. While "falling in love" is wonderful, it cannot truly satisfy our hearts—that only comes when we take love to the next level, intentionally loving whether we "feel in love" or not.

We must choose the hard work of learning to love each other with an authentic love—the sober-in-the-light-of-day love with or without the euphoria of the "in love" cover-of-night obsession. Authentic love, like a fine wine, will continue to grow and mature and improve over time, while the euphoria of romantic love will fade and wilt like a bouquet of cut flowers.

You must be willing to work through your relationship *out of* love because of the love you fell *into* in the first place. That was only a seed. It must be cultivated—weeds will need to be pulled—it will need to be harvested and even after that there will be a threshing to separate the good from the bad. Anything worth having requires time, attention, and labor—whether it is a garden, ministry, business, or even a beautiful marriage relationship.

What was it that drew you to each other in the very beginning? Even if it was nothing but physical attraction, your marriage is not a mistake. Whatever God used to draw you to your spouse was not accidental or a miscalculation. You were drawn together for good things. Deep and lasting joy in marriage will only come when you put your own needs, wants, and desires aside to work together toward something far greater and eternally more significant.

Every human being has weaknesses, flaws, and shortcomings. Marriage will expose those like no other relationship. God gave you a life partner to complete you. However, you will never be able to experience the joy and the peace in your marriage relationship that God has for you if you don't stay committed to it through "for better *and* for worse."

CHAPTER 3

MARRIAGE IS A COVENANT

Success in marriage does not come merely through finding the right mate, but through being the right mate. —Barnett R. Brickner

I have often said that you can eliminate your marriage, endure your marriage, or enjoy your marriage. While it is a sad fact that many would rather eliminate their marriages than endure them—it is just as sad still that many endure their marriages when they could be enjoying them. Marriage was designed so that in every endeavor we would be able to partner with someone special for as long as we live. It was created so that we could experience the deep and abiding satisfaction of fully trusting and being fully trusted by another—of fully knowing and being fully known—of being completely and unconditionally loved. It is the closest thing we will come to experiencing paradise on earth—of walking naked and unashamed with another human being.

Marriage was designed so that in every endeavor we would be able to partner with someone special for as long we live.

Marriage was designed as the fundamental building block of society. Because of its primary importance, God wants you to find a lasting fulfillment and stability in your marriage that will touch the lives of everyone you meet.

Regardless of how many books you've read on the subject, or seminars you've attended, you will not experience the fullness God intends for your marriage unless you *and* your spouse are committed to marriage as it was originally designed to be. The marriage "contract" demands loyalty, forbearance, self-denial, forgiveness, patience, and perseverance, just to name a few of the traits necessary to its success. In fact, calling it a "contract" doesn't really do it justice. It is not something designed to be embarked upon and then dissolved as if it were a simple merger between parties. It is not like sewing two pieces of cloth together to make a garment, where the stitching can later be removed and the two pieces separated again without much damage; it is more that the lives and hearts involved are knit or woven together so that it is hard to see where one begins and the other ends. There is no easy way to divide them without everything coming unraveled.

While in a contractual arrangement you seek to defend your rights and limit your responsibilities, in a covenant you surrender your rights and accept your responsibilities.

Because of that, I don't like to think of marriage as a contract, but prefer to use an older word: *covenant.* This ancient rite of joining tribes or families is what marriage is really all about and is the best example I can find of what we should each promise to the other when we get married. Unlike a contract, a covenant goes beyond a piece of paper you sign and date. While in a contractual arrangement you seek to defend your rights and limit your responsibilities, in a covenant you surrender your rights and accept your responsibilities. While contracts are made in the legal realm of do's and don'ts, a covenant involves a person's entire being—it is an arrangement entered into between two people requiring physical, emotional, spiritual, and intellectual commitments.

A contract is bound by certain time parameters, while a covenant is eternal, multigenerational, and even multidimensional.

In other words, while a contract is a natural, temporal device used to bind various parties within specific legal parameters, a covenant pledges hearts to be bound for life no matter what the circumstances. It is supernatural in that it supersedes the physical, law-bound realm arbitrated by human beings, and is instead mediated by God. Simply put, where a contract is legally binding, a covenant is spiritually binding.

Simply put, where a contract is legally binding, a covenant is spiritually binding.

A Brief History of Marriage

Forging covenants have always entailed more than simply signing documents with the formal proceedings of a treaty; it has historically involved a set of rituals and symbolic acts, the glimmer of which still exist in our marriage ceremonies and traditional wedding vows today. Taking a look at them can give us insight into what the marriage commitment truly represents. The *agape* love discussed in the last chapter was at the center of covenant relationship. It was the commitment of one covenant partner toward the other and was exemplified in the following ten exchanges and expressions of commitment.

One: The Exchanging of Gifts

The giving of gifts represents the giving of self. In the case of marriage, the gifts exchanged are rings. Prior to the wedding, there is usually an engagement ring given signifying the promise of marriage and therefore of being exclusively bound to one another. When two people become engaged they enter into a covenant of betrothal, or being formally betrothed. This word is derived from the Old English word *treuthe,* meaning "of a truth"—or "in good faith." It is a promise that each will be faithful and truthful to the other.

During the wedding ceremony, wedding rings are exchanged as a sign of this covenant commitment in front of witnesses to spiritually and communally seal what has already been decided in the heart. The symbol of the ring represents a binding together of two hearts without beginning or end—each heart being encircled or enveloped by the *agape* love of the other. Why the third finger on the left hand? Because it was once believed that the third finger contained the vein or artery that ran directly to the heart. Since the heart is positioned a little toward the left inside of the chest, the left hand is thus closer to the heart, so it was chosen over the right hand.

The giving of rings primarily represents an exchange of authority and a surrendering of self—spirit, soul, and body—or if you want to follow the love commitments of the last chapter, to love with *agape, phileo,* and *eros* in their highest and best forms. The apostle Paul wrote about the physical and spiritual nature of surrendering one's authority in the context of marriage in First Corinthians 7:3-4:

Let the husband render to his wife the affection due her, and likewise also the wife to her husband. The wife does not have authority over her own body, but the husband does. And likewise the husband does not have authority over his own body, but the wife does. (1 Corinthians 7:3-4)

Husbands and wives should be willing to fully give themselves to one another, not withholding any benefits of covenant, whether sexual, emotional, or spiritual. There should be no secrets or barriers between them. Like Adam and Eve, they should be completely transparent with each other—naked, unashamed, and unafraid. (And once again, this is about what you give to the other, not what you try to demand from one another.)

Two: The Exchange of Weapons

Exchanging weapons signified the commitment of both parties to offer their strength in protection of the other. In ancient times the two covenant partners would give each other their belts, scabbards, and swords symbolizing "my armaments are now your protection." This type of exchange was particularly meaningful because it signified a type of "covering"—the weakness of one party being covered by the strength of the other and vice versa.

This is what we see in the marriage as well—where men and women offer their complementary strengths to make up for each other's weaknesses. The idea that "your battles are my battles; your enemies are my enemies" is what the covenant relationship is all about, as well as the idea that "we will have each other's backs no matter what we face."

In the wedding ceremony, we promise to stand by one another through sickness and health, through poverty and wealth, "for better or for worse." This acknowledges how we know problems will surely come, but also that they will not alter our commitment to one another. Husbands and wives should protect and encourage each other, not be the prime inflictor of pain or frustration as seems so commonplace today. We should stand with our mate against his or her enemies, especially if that "enemy" is his or her own self. When they fail, we need to let them know, "If you make a mistake, I will still be by your side. If you fall, I will help you up."

To this end, the Bible calls on husbands to be the leaders of the family, but not the tyrant. As such, the husband is also the protector—meaning he should not be the one the wife has to be protected from! Leadership doesn't mean you have to run everything, but that you should be the one starting the conversations and making decisions that recognize your wife's strengths as well as vulnerabilities. It is a bit like leading on the dance floor—while the husband leads, he does it in such a way that everyone in the room is focused on how beautiful and graceful his wife is, not on how wonderful he is. He simply provides the frame that protects and showcases the abilities of his wife. The better she looks, the better he's doing his job!

The wife, on the other hand, is the heart of the family. As the heart, you could say she pumps blood into the arms that are holding her up—the life force that gives her husband the courage and confidence he needs to be a good leader. Husbands have a deep need to be respected and admired by their wives, confident that they are being supported against whatever they may face. The wife's respect will empower and strengthen the husband to be bolder and more confident in broadening the family's influence and estate.

Nothing undermines a husband's strength faster than a wife who belittles him, treats him like he can't handle the job, or who tears him down in front of relatives or friends. When a wife or husband attacks the other, they are really undermining themselves, though it is a cycle that very few seem to recognize. The dance of marriage tends to have more missteps if it is not done with the confidence that comes with each edifying the other. Obviously both need to feel the love, support, and respect of their spouse.

Nothing undermines a husband's strength faster than a wife who belittles him, treats him like he can't handle the job, or who tears him down in front of relatives or friends.

Your mate should never wonder if you are on his or her side. Support one another in public and work out your differences privately—and by all means, do not tear each other down in front of your children. Whatever you do in view of your kids will be teaching them how to treat their spouses in the future.

Remember, your strengths are there to inspire one another, not to impose your will on each other. Commitment in covenant means you are more concerned with how you support, protect, and nurture your spouse than whether your own rights and needs are being fulfilled.

Three: The Sacrifice of an Animal

In ancient times, the sacrificial offering of an animal represented the sacrificial offering of one's assets to provide for the other. In Genesis 15, when Abraham first entered into a covenant with God, he sacrificed a cow, a goat, and a sheep. *"So Abram…killed them. Then he cut each animal down the middle and laid the halves side by side"* (Gen. 15:10 NLT). It was also a way of saying, "May all that I have be divided like this if I ever break this agreement." He walked between the pieces saying, "This animal represents me; I die to myself and my old life." From the most ancient of times, this was part of the covenant-sealing ritual.

In addition, the sacrificial death of the animal signified the commitment "until death do us part." A blood covenant can only end with the death of a partner, but even then the heirs were often honor bound to continue it. We see this in Second Samuel 9 when David welcomes Mephibosheth to live in his house and eat always at his table for the sake of David's covenant with Mephibosheth's father, Jonathan. As David put it, *"Is there still anyone left of the house of Saul, that I may show him kindness for Jonathan's sake?"* (2 Sam. 9:1 ESV).

Four: The Mingling of Blood

The mingling of blood signifies the exchanging of lives—that the two lives are now one—because blood represents life. If you grew up watching old westerns as I did, you saw this again and again when two men would cut their palms and then clasp hands, mingling the blood and thus becoming "blood brothers." Without the shedding of blood, there is no blood covenant.

We fulfill this step in marriage when the husband and wife consummate the marriage and the virgin woman, through the breaking of the hymen, sheds blood. Jewish parents of the groom received a special cloth upon which the bride's blood was spilled as proof that the marriage covenant had been sealed. This also signifies how we were meant to enter such a covenant only once. While we don't do that today, the honeymoon is still the time for the newlywed husband and wife to get away together in a special time of celebrating and consummating their marriage relationship.

Hebrews 13:4 in The Message says we should *"Honor marriage, and guard the sacredness of sexual intimacy between wife and husband. God draws a firm line against casual and illicit sex."* While the marriage bed is pure and "undefiled" in God's sight, sex outside of marriage is extremely offensive to God. Engaging in sex with unmarried partners makes a mockery of the beautiful sacramental role sex has within the marriage covenant. This sacred intimacy is required to bridge the common breaches or complete the regular healing necessary in a marriage relationship. If one party cannot freely give themselves to the other, then the heart may still be holding onto an offense. Withholding oneself physically is often a sign that one is also withholding his or her heart.

If one party cannot freely give themselves to the other, then the heart may still be holding onto an offense.

Five: The Exchanging of Names

Covenant partners commit to upholding the honor of each other's name by receiving the name of the other. That is why you will see hyphenated names among nobility in Europe—at some point two "houses" or families covenanted together. Today, the woman traditionally takes the name of the man. To share a name is to share the character and reputation of the other person. Your identity is wrapped up in the identity of your spouse—whatever you say or do will reflect on the character of your covenant partner. Because your behavior will have an effect on how others see your spouse, be careful not to bring shame or embarrassment on him or her. Their honor is in your keeping when you share their name or they share yours.

Because your behavior will have an effect on how others see your spouse, be careful not to bring shame or embarrassment on him or her.

Six: The Creation of a Scar

In older times, a scar would have been cut where we wear a wedding ring today. This visible evidence is a public statement that two people belong to each other. This is why we invite witnesses to the ceremony and file a document with government authorities—it is a mark of our covenant with one another before the world. Witnesses to the ceremony were expected to help those in the covenant keep it.

Community has always been of vital importance in the sight of God. A person attracted to another who sees the "mark" of the ring should honor their covenant and not try to tempt him or her to compromise their commitment. Today, when someone wants to be unfaithful to their husband or wife, they simply slip off their ring. That is something that should never happen.

Seven: The Recitation of Vows

The part of covenant that most carries over into today's wedding ceremonies is the exchanging of vows. When we exchange vows, we are exchanging promises to love, honor, and respect one another, and to share all things in common—including hardships. Once married, everything should be shared equally such as all wealth and all debts. If you possess property before marriage that you are not willing to share with your spouse, then don't get married! You share all things in common, the good and the bad—the assets as well as the debts. As covenant partners, it is together that you will find the strength and resources necessary to overcome any obligations to outside parties.

We see this problem more and more today as husbands and wives more commonly divide their finances by having their own accounts and separate assets. They may even sign a prenuptial agreement. In my opinion, a prenuptial agreement is nothing more than a pre-divorce arrangement. If this is your attitude, then you don't have a covenant heart. Remember that "liabilities" also include shortcomings and weaknesses. You should give grace to your spouse in their weakness just as God extends grace to you.

Eight: The Breaking of Bread

Covenant-makers have historically broken bread together. This is what Jesus did at the Last Supper and is remembered in the sacrament of Christian Communion today. Breaking bread in this way made the statement, "This is my body, broken for you. The strength of my body is yours." As the two parties served one another wine, they made the statement, "This is my blood, my life, which I will spend in blessing you." This concept did not originate with Jesus at the Passover Supper before His crucifixion. It was always part of the covenant ritual from the days of Abraham.

Symbolically, breaking bread and sharing a meal signifies that, "I am in you and you are in me." The effect of covenant is that it causes two to become one. The remnant of this in today's wedding ceremony is when the bride and groom feed wedding cake to each other. Today this is usually done in jest, smearing food on each other, ignorant of the beautiful symbolism this act represents. Unfortunately, many couples today go on from this to "smear" each other in their private and public lives as well, never realizing they are on the same side, but instead blaming all of their failures on the other.

Nine: The Planting of a Memorial

The planting of a memorial was a common practice when trees or fields were planted in honor of a newly formed covenant, or altars or some other stone structure was erected as a memorial. The "planting" of a memorial is completed in the context of a marriage when the seed of the man is planted inside the womb of the woman and a child comes forth. Children are permanent reminders of the marriage covenant—they are also the perpetuators of the covenant. The child is the "memorial" in which all generations will know a covenant of love existed between the parents.

Ten: Calling Each Other "Friend"

The term "friend" was used to describe covenant partners and meant much more than it does today. So when Jesus said to His disciples, *"I no longer call you servants...I have called you friends"* (see John 15:15 NIV), this was a way of saying, "I am always for you—all that I am and have is yours." A husband and wife should be one another's best friend in much the same way. This kind of *friend:*

- Loves faithfully regardless of mistakes.
- Gives all and withholds nothing.
- Doesn't reject or withhold love because one or the other fails in some way.
- Values and upholds the relationship against all other things.
- Isn't preoccupied with making the partner become what you need, but is occupied with how to love that person faithfully and supply whatever he or she needs.

Working Love Into the "Process"

Thus you see that entering into covenant relationship and "becoming one" was a process. In ancient times, when a couple entered into marriage, it was not just a 20-minute ceremony. The covenant relationship actually began when the groom proposed. It was during the proposal that the groom would present a cup of wine to be shared with his intended bride signifying their entrance into a blood covenant.

After the marriage covenant had been established, there would be a year of separation before the groom and his escorts would come for the bride, usually in a formal procession that took place in the evening. The bride and her attendants would have been prepared for the groom's unannounced arrival by keeping their lamps perpetually lit. As the groom approached, he would shout out to alert the bridal party that he had come to escort them to his father's house.

The groom would not come for the bride until the bridal chamber he had prepared for her was ready—and the only person who could determine its readiness was the groom's father. When the groom was asked when he would retrieve his bride, he would commonly say, "Only my father knows." After the bridal chamber had been declared ready, the groom would retrieve the bride from her home and escort her to the house of his father where the wedding guests would be assembled.

Not long after their arrival, the bride and groom would enter the wedding chamber where they would consummate the marriage. It was after the marriage union had been consummated that the celebration would begin and then continue for seven days. But it would not end there. The time allotted by law for the honeymoon was one full year.

When a man has taken a new wife, he shall not go out to war or be charged with any business; he shall be free at home one year, and bring happiness to his wife whom he has taken (Deuteronomy 24:5).

"Let the wife make the husband glad to come home, and let him make her sorry to see him leave."

Establishing a marriage covenant was a significant event that required the undivided attention of both parties for at least two years—the first year, while the bride was diligent to keep her lamp burning, the groom was building the wedding chamber. After the wedding, the husband was home with his wife with the only imperative of making her happy. As Martin Luther put it, "Let the wife make the husband glad to come home, and let him make her sorry to see him leave."[1] Surprisingly, the burden of wedding preparations and the marital satisfaction to follow fell on the groom.

Endnote

1. http://www.brainyquote.com/quotes/authors/m/martin_luther_2.html (accessed June 15, 2010).

CHAPTER 4

BECOMING ONE FLESH

Happy marriages begin when we marry the ones we love, and they blossom when we love the ones we marry. —Tom Mullen

Thus, as an occasion for covenant making, marriage connected many aspects of society. It marked new alliances between families, the merging of financial assets, commitment to the stability of the local community, and the linking of destinies. In that day and age, marriages were often arranged between families for any numbers of reasons, and romantic love was very seldom considered an important element to initiate a marriage. Couples would learn to love each other as the years went along, and if romantic love just happened to be present, that was a wonderful bonus. However, being in or out of love had very little to do with staying married.

While arranged marriages reflect a tradition seldom practiced in the world today, they are still worthy of note because of their relative success—due largely in part because they were based on *loving* each other even if the feeling of romantic love was not there. It was a covenant/*agape* relationship.

While such marriages were sometimes endured for the sake of keeping together all they joined, today marriages are broken up without a thought for anything but the fickle "happiness" of one of the partners. The husband or wife will feel a sense of dissatisfaction with their relationship—especially dangerous in a society where anything less than satisfaction is rarely tolerated—and because they are no longer "in love" think the best way forward for everyone is divorce. Little thought is given to the lasting impact such a decision will have on their children, their respective families, their finances, or their communities.

The change in marriage was perhaps no more dramatically seen than in the last five decades starting right around the time that Billie and I were married. The 1970s saw the mass adoption of the no-fault divorce laws that we have today and with them the reasons getting divorced began to shift. Even as late as the 1950s and early 1960s, couples still considered marriage an institution for the greater good of society to which they had to stay married except under reasons of extreme duress or cruelty.

The laws of that day upheld that view as people had to prove a reason for divorce whether that be infidelity, abuse, abandonment, criminal activity, or some other serious violation of the marriage "contract." Marriage was even more costly and painful to the individuals involved than it is today, if that is possible to believe.

With the emphasis put on self-actualization and personal fulfillment that started in the 1970s, marriage slowly changed from something that was done for the sake of many different important components of society to something that was more about satisfying the desires and emotional needs of the two individuals who got married. Thus the bar was dropped on what qualified as a reason for divorce from a provable act of betrayal to things along the lines of "you just don't make me happy anymore."

Psychologists of the time even touted that divorce would make marriage stronger because it would weed out the weak marriages, and that divorce could very well be a psychologically responsible necessity for the health of society. The effects of divorce on the children were downplayed as in theory there would be ample replacements for mother or father figures elsewhere. They argued that the opportunity to divorce if you were unhappy was actually an opportunity for the growth of everyone involved, and it became acceptable as a necessary step for people who needed to go out and "find themselves."

They argued that the opportunity to divorce if you were unhappy was actually an opportunity for the growth of everyone involved, and it became acceptable as a necessary step for people who needed to go out and "find themselves."

However, research in recent decades has shown just the opposite. Easier divorce has actually weakened the commitment to marriage rather than strengthened it. Convenient divorce made it common to question whether any current marriage provided the best life had to offer—it caused husbands and wives to ask, "Maybe I'd be happier right now with someone else?"

Around the same time, people began to accept the idea that they should live together first to see if they would ultimately be compatible. Statistics have shown, however, that the vast majority of those who live together are even less committed to staying together if they do go on to marry, let alone are happier in their marriages. In other words, living together before getting married does not improve a couple's degree of compatibility or level of commitment. Instead it just makes the partner seem even more "disposable."

Furthermore, children whose parents were divorced became nearly twice as likely to divorce themselves, as well as roughly three times more likely to drop out of school. Girls of divorced parents are three times more likely to become unwed mothers, and boys whose parents divorce are more than twice as likely to spend time in prison by the age of 32.

As one researcher speculated, if we had the same level of divorces today as in 1960, "the nation would have 750,000 fewer children repeating grades, 1.2 million fewer school suspensions, approximately 500,000 fewer acts of teenage delinquency, about 600,000 fewer kids receiving therapy, and approximately 70,000 fewer suicide attempts every year."[1] Another expert estimated that this family breakdown in America is costing the public roughly $112 billion a year in attorneys' fees, social services, and other government programs required to help single-parent families and children suffering from the effects as well as other societal costs.[2] While divorce rates are dropping in the United States,[3] the change is economically disproportional and contributes to the growing divide between the richer and poorer families of our nation.

As Billie and I counsel couples, we don't tell them they should stay together in a miserable marriage enduring the hardships for the sake of their kids, finances, communities, or any of the other elements that the marriage covenant merges together. What we do ask them to consider is whether they are willing to do the work of transforming their marriage for the sake of all these reasons. An unhappy marriage isn't to be endured "for the sake of the kids"—it needs to be transformed and healed.

Unless there is a situation of abuse, unrepentant infidelity or abandonment, or something of this nature, the best future for any nation is lasting marriages—and the best future for any marriage is a commitment by both spouses to do what is necessary to make the relationship a source of comfort and intimacy, not of contention and constant strife.

The important message we have to share with couples is that their issues *can* be worked through. Making a marriage work isn't as complicated as landing a person on the moon. There are things you can do to change the atmosphere of your home from a war zone into a peace zone of restoration, and most of them are so simple people tend to overlook them.

While we discuss these things more in the upcoming chapters, the thing you need to realize now is that they won't work if you aren't first committed and open to doing what it takes to *make* them work—and making them work together. You have to look at the cost to your own ego, desires, and habits and determine that no matter what the price, you will pay it, because your marriage—and your family and your kids—are worth it. Marriage only becomes the fulfillment it can be when you are committed to it no matter how you *feel*, and when you acknowledge that underneath it all, you have never really stopped loving your spouse. Then you will realize that your most fulfilling and happiest future has always been one that includes him or her.

So, Are You For or Against Your Spouse?

God designed us to satisfy one another's needs in relationship, not to be absorbed with our own. Marriage was never meant to descend into a tournament of selfishness where two people become perpetually dissatisfied and unfulfilled and try to manipulate one another to get what they want. Marriage is a sacrament, and as such it is meant to be a blessing to all involved.

Self is always the enemy that keeps us from a great marriage.

Self is always the enemy that keeps us from a great marriage. Everyone wants their own way—and too many of us are willing to put satisfying ourselves ahead of, or at the expense of, our spouses. Most of us have played the blame game of rationalizing and justifying our self-centered conduct for most of the life of our marriages. The world is always looking for an excuse to be relieved from the personal responsibility of making love-based choices.

If you gain nothing else from reading this book, I want you to remember that with a contract you *protect* your rights and *limit* your responsibilities, but with a covenant you *surrender* your rights and *accept* your responsibilities. Thus marriage is something that demands surrender and acceptance, something very difficult to do without the divine intervention of *agape* love.

This is why the Bible calls marriage a great mystery (see Eph. 5:32). The principle of "oneness" it uses to describe the covenant relationship is what makes it more powerfully binding than any legal contract—yet it is not an instrument of bondage, but of freedom. It is not about living up to the expectations of another and meeting their every whim, it is about giving yourself completely for their benefit—more succinctly put, it is about what you give to the other, not what they give to you.

As mentioned previously, in a contract, the two separate parties hold one another accountable for meeting obligations. Each party has entered into a legally binding arrangement to get something of benefit from the other in exchange for certain compensations. It is a "take-take" rather than a "give-give" arrangement—and that is why all it will ever be is "an arrangement."

A covenant, on the other hand, holds at its heart the continuing, evolving relationship. Contracts don't really have the leeway to adapt over time without being changed and updated; covenants are about being benevolent no matter what the changes and new phases of life may bring.

If a marriage is going to work and is going to last—if we're going to get married and stay married—then the marriage has to be made up of two people who are willing to surrender their rights and accept their responsibilities. This is a matter of the heart and the will more than it is of the mind or emotions. The challenges, the struggles, and the adversities we encounter in marriage relations are common to all married couples—and can only be resolved with a renewal and change of the heart. When you maintain your car, you've got to do more than fill it with oil—you've got to *change* the oil. You need to replace the dirty oil with clean oil. As David often prayed, *"Create in me a clean heart, O God, and renew a right spirit within me"* (Ps. 51:10 ESV), so should you and I.

Sadly, we have seen too many couples spend their lives together *regulating* their relationship challenges, regulating the way they talk to each other, and regulating what they do around difficult issues instead of *resolving* them. The reason why the same challenges continue to come up time and again is because we are in the habit of giving into the convenience of regulation rather than doing the challenging work of resolution. We regulate how we think and how we react—we regulate our emotions—but we fail to do the deeper work of surrendering our hearts.

These recurring issues are spiritual in nature and therefore must be resolved on a spiritual level—on the level of the heart rather than the "who's right/who's wrong" level of the mind. Spiritual issues of the heart cannot be resolved by intellectualizing, over-analyzing, or some other mental gymnastics. We have seen that most struggling couples need to get out of their heads and back into their hearts.

If you are like most husbands and wives, you believe your spouse is the problem. With genuine sincerity, you believe that if only your spouse would change, you *and* your spouse would be happier. You only want the best for your marriage, and if your spouse would step up to the plate and do his or her part, things would be better. The truth of the matter is that if your spouse changed you would still not be happy, because your spouse is not the issue. You are the issue. You are the challenge. You are the problem, because ultimately you can only control what *you* do. Of course the flip side of that is the good news— *you* are also the *solution*.

While everything our spouses do will affect us, we do not have to allow ourselves to become infected with bitterness, unforgiveness, hatred, or a retaliatory spirit. Everything that Billie does affects me and everything I do *affects* her; however, we do not have to allow what the other does to *infect* us with negativity. This is where we must learn to take responsibility.

How committed are you to making your marriage work and keeping the home fires of your love burning? Which do you hope to do for the remainder of your lifetime: eliminate your marriage, endure your marriage, or enjoy your marriage? These can be tough questions to ask, but making things better in your marriage starts with your commitment to do so.

The realization that putting aside doing things your way for your own benefit is crucial if you are going to see real change. But that is also where true love starts, and that selfless love is what makes all the difference. You must put eliminating or enduring your marriage in the rear-view mirror and go on to really enjoying a growing intimacy together—beyond even what you experienced during the days of your first love.

Endnotes

1. W. Bradford Wilcox, "The Evolution of Divorce," *National Affairs* magazine, Fall 2009, http://nationalaffairs.com/publications/detail/the-evolution-of-divorce#bottom%20correction (accessed: April 24, 2010).

2. Erin Roach, "Family Breakdown Costs Taxpayers," *The Christian Index,* June 19, 2008, http://www.christianindex.org/4545.article (accessed June 15, 2010).

3. "Divorce Rates Drop to Lowest Since 1970," *USA Today,* May 1, 2007, http://www.usatoday.com/news/nation/2007-05-11-divorce-decline_N.htm (accessed June 15, 2010).

CHAPTER 5

GOD'S ULTIMATE INTENTION: INTIMACY

Oh, the comfort—the inexpressible comfort of feeling safe with a person—having neither to weigh thoughts nor measure words, but pouring them all right out, just as they are, chaff and grain together; certain that a faithful hand will take and sift them, keep what is worth keeping, and then with the breath of kindness blow the rest away.
—Dinah Craik, *A Life for a Life,* 1859

Marriage was created for communion—for the common union of two people, two lives, and two destinies. It was not created for economic or social stability, emotional or physical gratification, or even for the perpetuation of the human race—though these are wonderful by-products of healthy marriages—as much as for the purpose of sharing intimacy.

Marriage exemplifies God's heart for humanity. Intimacy is at the center of oneness.

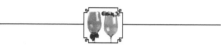

God's desire for intimacy is a core theme woven into the very concept of covenant.

God's desire for intimacy is a core theme woven into the very concept of covenant. Covenant cannot exist without intimacy and true intimacy cannot exist without the total commitment of a covenant. When God said, "the two shall become one," He wasn't just talking about coming together sexually and producing children. Sexual desire and romantic love may well be driving forces behind why we want to get married in the first place, but ultimately it is emotional, intellectual, and spiritual intimacy that brings meaning and fulfillment to the marriage union.

Think back to when you were dating for a moment. What were the most memorable times? Certainly you had fun doing things together, from going to movies to football games to formal events, but the joy of dating was the talking, getting to know each other, and opening up your hearts to one another. Billie and I spent hours talking in the weeks we were dating and all it did was cause us to fall more and more madly in love.

When you spend time talking and sharing like this—about your childhood, your dreams, your ambitions, passions, and thoughts on whatever topic—slowly you pull back the veil on your soul and personality, revealing just a little bit more of who you really are as you observe how the other reacts. As you learn that each part of you is being accepted without hesitation, you begin to share a little more, and the feeling of love between you grows.

However, should you sense resistance or rejection on some level, you will begin to withhold yourself, and if that continues, you will eventually end the dating relationship to look for someone else with whom to share your life. This is the innate need for intimacy that is within all of us—something I would describe as the need to be fully known and fully loved at the same time. If this process continues, we get to the point where we feel we can share our whole hearts with the other person—even though we really haven't yet—and we feel comfortable with the idea of marrying and binding our futures together spirit, soul, and body.

Some would say discovering our purpose or giving our lives for the greater good meets our innate need for meaning, but I believe it is in the achieving of true intimacy—a sense of *oneness* with that *one* (not two or three or four) other person. Oneness, as we have seen, is a sharing of our lives on all levels—a deep and abiding intimacy on every level and in every realm of life.

Intimacy is achieved through an authentic and transparent sharing and accepting of one another. That kind of togetherness defies natural law and natural understanding, because it takes something more than we know on our own. While it demands that we surrender ourselves, it is also about giving, trusting, and empowering the other person in the relationship. It is what marriage was designed to be—to intimately create life together as we partner in every aspect of life.

Love and Intimacy

Intimacy is a oneness of purpose and of the heart—it means to be fully known and fully loved by one special person who you give your all to fully support. If two become one in this way, then they are joined together in all areas. It does not mean that they become the same person or carbon copies of each other, but they will have the same goals, plans, and ambitions in each of the realms of life: the spiritual, emotional, intellectual, professional, financial, social, and physical. The most important aspect of this oneness is the communication—or exchange—that goes on between the two—an exchange that is never healthy if each person in the relationship is not healthy and balanced regarding who they are as individuals first.

Intimacy isn't so much the act of being seen, as it is the act of seeing.

I've often heard *intimacy* defined as "into-me-see." It is a complete transparency with the other person, which takes honest sharing and years of trust. While most people think of sex when they think of intimacy, true intimacy is really a matter of the heart and soul. But keep in mind that intimacy isn't so much the act of *being* seen, as it is the act of *seeing*. It is intentionally and proactively looking deeply into the heart of the other—a willingness to be open to what the other is seeing—yielding yourself to experience what the other is experiencing, and understanding that which the other understands from their perspective outside of your own. It is looking into each other's lives with forgiveness, empathy, and unconditional love.

Jesus did this when He suffered on behalf of humanity. Because He left His heavenly domain to live on this earth as a human being, Jesus is able to relate with us on every level. *"Jesus understands every weakness of ours, because He was tempted in every way that we are…"* (Heb. 4:15 CEV). Jesus is a personal witness of the weakness of our selfish natures as much as we are a witness of His moral strength—and because He has witnessed our pain and suffering, we are able to bear witness of His power to heal, deliver, save, and forgive.

Our personal witness is what gives us right standing before God. Until we can personally bear witness of Christ's saving work of grace—we will never be recipients of His strength to overcome our own selfish desires. Because we have "bore witness" of Him, we are able to stand upright in His Presence—naked and unashamed. I firmly believe there is no genuine intimacy in life without knowing God, for it is only as we come to God and give our lives to Jesus that we are in fact fully known and fully loved. Until we know such openness, such intimacy, and such unconditional, forgiving love, how do we ever think we can share that with another?

Our openness before Jesus gives us entrance into God's inner chamber where every aspect of our "self" is examined, forgiven, healed, and transformed. There is no greater intimacy. As we go through this process before God, we gain the confidence to live fully as who He created us to be, bold and unashamed. This realization should transform every relationship in our lives, but most notably our marriages. Our spouse can then become a witness to our lives, someone who can wholeheartedly share this wonderful adventure with us—someone who can know the worst thing about us and love us in spite of it.

Whatever we go through, good or bad, having someone to share it with makes for "double the joy and half the sorrow." The famous anthropologist, Margaret Mead, said, "Having someone wonder where you are when you don't come home at night is a very old human need."[1] People were not wired to spend their lives alone. In the movie *Shall We Dance?* with Richard Gere, Susan Sarandon, and Jennifer Lopez, the daughter asked her mother, played by Sarandon, why people got married. She replies:

> We need a witness to our lives. There's a billion people on the planet…. I mean, what does any one life really mean? But in a marriage, you're promising to care about everything. The good things, the bad things, the terrible things, the mundane things…all of it, all of the time, every day. You're saying "Your life will not go unnoticed because I will notice it. Your life will not go unwitnessed because I will be your witness."

We all need someone to witness our lives—somebody to witness that we had worth, we had value, we made a difference, and that we were compassionate and made a contribution to the world, even if it was only a small one.

I believe that is remarkably insightful. We all need someone to witness our lives—somebody to witness that we had worth, we had value, we made a difference, and that we were compassionate and made a contribution to the world, even if it was only a small one. We need someone who will know us down to our very worst faults, and then love us anyway.

Endnote

1. http://www.brainyquote.com/quotes/authors/m/margaret_mead_2.html (accessed June 15, 2010).

CHAPTER 6

TRIANGLE OF HOPE

You can never be happily married to another until you get a divorce from yourself. Successful marriage demands a certain death to self. —Jerry McCant

When Billie and I counsel with a couple, one of the first things we do—after we've done a good deal of listening—is explain what the marriage relationship was really meant to look like in the first place. We talk about covenant—as we have already done in a previous chapter—about the critical importance of surrendering rights and accepting responsibilities. Without first understanding this basic principle, getting to the finer points of intimacy will be impossible. As we talk about what true intimacy looks like, and how to achieve it, I'll begin to explain what I call the "Triangle of Hope."

Taking a pencil and paper, I draw a triangle. The three points represent the three entities of which every marriage is comprised: the husband, the wife, and God. At each bottom corner of the triangle, in their two respective places, are the husband and wife—at the apex, or at the top of the triangle, is God. As the husband and wife move toward each other along the bottom, they come to an impenetrable wall that cannot be breached. They cannot go around it, they cannot go under or over it, and they certainly cannot break through it.

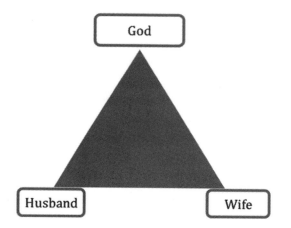

Take a look at the diagram for a moment. You will see a vertical line that goes from the top of the triangle to the bottom, separating the husband and wife. As they move toward each other to enjoy the intimacy they both long for, they encounter this as an impassable wall. I call this wall the "self-me-my-I" barrier, because it is really our own inability to escape the selfish desires and hidden motives in our lives. It is the part of us that plots and schemes to get what we want from the other without giving up too much of ourselves. It is the culprit that undermines marriage and intimacy because of fear, pride, shame, feelings of inferiority, memories of past painful events, abusive behavior patterns, or any number of other issues and weaknesses.

This barrier separates husband and wife from one another because each, whether they want to or not, can't help but consider their own feelings first—putting their own needs, wants, and desires before those of their spouse. For most of us, we don't even realize this wall is there, or that it is there because of what we are withholding from our spouse, not the other way around.

Usually we are thinking, "He/she is not meeting my needs," "He always.../she never...," or "She/he never really listens to me." We may even have convinced ourselves that we are putting the other first in everything, but when it comes down to seeing how we behave from day to day, our actions and attitudes tell a different story. We have never fully trusted the other with who we are, and then project the shortcomings in the relationship onto them instead of accepting the responsibility for addressing the real problem—which is firmly within ourselves.

After running into this barrier again and again, eventually, in frustration, most husbands and wives withdraw, giving up on intimacy as being achievable, and complacently coexist rather than actively partnering together in the various aspects of life. Trust wanes, we start to focus on what is easier and more controllable like how we perform at work, what we do with our friends, or else we get lost in our hobbies.

We begin the process of *regulating* our behaviors in our own separate quadrants instead of *resolving* the issues that tear down "the wall." Each difference of opinion over key issues of your future together, every decision to "agree to disagree," everything you quietly blame on the other or sweep under the rug is like adding another layer of bricks to "the wall." As we do, the "self-me-my-I" wall grows stronger and thicker, and we grow increasingly distant from one another. Eventually, we open ourselves up to the thoughts that lead to divorce: "This relationship isn't meeting my needs—I deserve better than this! I will never be happy in this marriage—what's the point of staying together?" Notice again all of the "I," "I," "I" statements.

When you are intimate, these conversations should build up walls of protection *around* you as a couple, not *between* you. Every time you resolve an issue rather than regulating how you react to one another, it binds you closer together creating a protective barrier between your marriage and any outside forces—or internal thoughts—that would threaten to erode it. Making a choice to respond to God and resolve the issues rather than react to each other and regulate behavior is the key to victory.

Making a choice to respond to God and resolve the issues rather than react to each other and regulate behavior is the key to victory.

While the couple may participate in a marriage seminar to learn how to better relate to each other, this doesn't break down the "self-me-my-I" wall. That doesn't mean I think marriage seminars are bad, but very seldom do they ever address the real issue that divides couples—and virtually all of the wisdom they share will have no effect until the "self-me-my-I" wall is dealt with. If it is not, all they will learn at a seminar are psychological techniques to enable them to more effectively manipulate their spouse to get what they want—to eek out of the other person what they feel they need while only appearing to give back to their spouses themselves.

As the husband and wife learn to apply more advanced techniques in regulating the other, they head toward each other again, but no matter how many times or how hard they try to breach the "self-me-my-I" wall, they still won't get through it. They will never escape "self" to have true intimacy with each other until they learn how to tear down that wall.

Billie and I have found that for the first seven, eight, sometimes ten years of marriage, couples manage to get along with each well enough from their respective sides of this wall. They learn to tolerate each other and regulate the issues they face without ever really having to deal with them. That's what my parents did for a lifetime. They never resolved the root issues that were between them and simply coexisted. Billie and I determined some years into our marriage we would not do that. We committed ourselves to dealing with the foundational issues of the "self-me-my-I" barrier.

However, for a long time, we didn't succeed. Then at some point, we both came to the conclusion that we couldn't please the other no matter what we did. Eventually each of us thought, "You know what, I can't make this marriage work. No matter what I do, there is something keeping me from really connecting. God, help me! I can't go on living like this. Lord, what am I supposed to do?" As we did this, we each began to head up our respective side of the triangle toward God asking Him to rule over our hearts, lead us and guide us, and change us so that we could really walk in love. Day by day, we continued to pursue God's wisdom, and day by day, God started to teach us what we needed to know to have the intimacy with one another we were longing for.

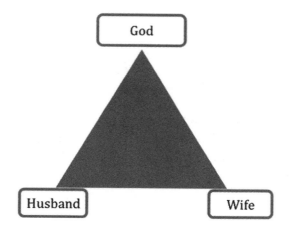

If you get frustrated enough and fall on your knees before God, He will become your personal life coach and advisor—He will take over the helm of your heart and mind and start steering the ship of your marriage into a safe and peaceful harbor with your mate.

As Billie and I chased after God for the answer, we were able to peel back layer after layer of our lives and hearts before Him and one another, and began to experience the kind of intimacy God had always intended for our marriage. He loved us, forgave us, and healed us in spite of who we were. As we each grew closer to God, we began to get closer to each other as well. "But what about the 'self-me-my-I' barrier?" you may ask. Well, it began to slowly crumble. You see, as we allowed God to help us break down the selfish barriers between ourselves and Himself, He showed us how to break through our own "self-me-my-I" barriers to be more intimate with each other. As He expressed His love for us despite our shortcomings and idiosyncrasies, we were able to start overcoming the small hurts and slights we felt from each other and love each other unconditionally as He did us.

You see, if Jesus Christ gave His life *for* you to give His life *to* you to live His life *through* you, what do you think is bound to happen? Your selfishness will begin to weaken as you become stronger and more confident on the inside—you will begin to not need to take from others so much and suddenly have things to give instead. Do you see how that can begin to change a marriage?

First Things First

This is the heart of covenant commitment. When we pledge so much to the benefit of the other in covenant, we need supernatural help to be able to follow through on our promise. Telling the other they can depend on us makes us more dependant on God.

If Billie and I are both hanging out at the top of the triangle with Jesus and being filled with and guided by His love, then we will love each other all that much better, we will know ourselves that much better, see the selfishness and pettiness that are at the foundation of the "self-me-my-I" wall, and begin to dismantle it brick by brick. Only then will we begin to experience the intimacy and oneness in our relationship we both wanted all along.

If we start to walk away from God, however, we also walk away from each other. If one of us walks away from God, it doesn't matter how closely the other is walking with God, it won't solve the problem of selfishness that will creep back into the other person's life. Each one of us must make the decision to pursue God and love Him with all of our hearts, souls, minds, and strength on our own—and until we do that, we will never be able to love another person as much as we do ourselves. It is a classic formula that those who don't know God never understand: $1 + 1 + 1 = 1$. As we find intimacy with God, we find intimacy with each other, and the three together become one in spirit and purpose.

The cause of our relationship problems will always be rooted in our lack of relationship with God.

The cause of our relationship problems will always be rooted in our lack of relationship with God. If you want greater intimacy in your marriage, you must first seek greater intimacy with Him. Until you love Christ first and foremost, you won't be able to love your wife or serve your husband as Jesus loves and serves His people.

This was what I began to realize that day on my knees in the gutter of Main Street in Victoria, Texas. I needed to be delivered of a violent, hard drinking, self-absorbed *me* before I could ever love Billie as she deserved. I was madly in love with her on the inside, but that love wasn't breaking through the "self-me-my-I" barrier. Only God could break the bondage my past was holding me in at that time; and in order for me to live that freedom day by day, I had to seek God for it day by day. Sadly, it took many difficult years before this became a reality in my life.

As we counsel couples, we watch this happen all of the time. One spouse will back away from God, and no matter how closely the other is walking with Jesus, no matter how much he or she loves, honors, respects, or submits to the other, the self-seeking spouse will gradually be so blinded by their own selfishness that they will think the other person is the problem, not them. They will grow more and more frustrated, impatient, angry, and dissatisfied with the other trying to change them, never recognizing it is actually they themselves who need to change.

The further we grow away from God, the more powerful a grip selfishness has upon us, and the more toxic it is to the intimacy we desire in our marriage.

This is the essence of what we're trying to convey in this book. After 44 years of marriage, we have found that the only way we have ever really been able to resolve our issues with each other is at the feet of Jesus. When we *resolve* them with Him first, only then can we begin to communicate effectively and truly *resolve* our differences with one another.

This is very different from the *regulating* that sweeps things under the rug to the point that there is eventually a mountain of unresolved issues dividing us. Only by resolving the issues that arise daily can we begin to experience intimacy every day. *The heart of the problem is always a problem of the heart.* The cure for spiritual heart disease is always more of God—a love transfusion created by transplanting His heart into the place of our dead, cold hearts of stone.

I believe that covenant begins with God, and then is shared with each other.

I believe that covenant begins with God, and then is shared with each other.

The Book of Second Samuel tells the story of King David when he saw Bathsheba bathing on a nearby rooftop and fell "in love" with her to the point he committed adultery with her so that she became pregnant, and then had her husband killed so he could make her his wife in an attempt to cover it up (see 2 Sam. 11). After Nathan had confronted him about the sin, he didn't go to his counselors, his other wives, or even to the priest to seek forgiveness. Instead David fell to his knees and prayed to God, *"I have sinned against the Lord"* (2 Sam. 12:13). But didn't David feel he had sinned against Bathsheba and her husband, Uriah, or even against his other wives? How could he say that he had only sinned against God? Because his covenant is first and foremost with God, and his sorrow was based on his violation of God's trust more than what the consequences of his sin would be.

When David sinned, he disobeyed God and broke the foundational covenant upon which every covenant and commitment in his life was built. Godly sorrow is being more grieved about your sin against God than the consequences of your sin. That is true repentance. You can be sorry for what you do to other people, but it is first before God you must repent. Likewise, before you can truly be right with other people, you must be right with God. You can never see your sin against another until you see it against a Holy God first.

Godly sorrow is being more grieved about your sin against God than the consequences of your sin.

It's All Proportionate

How we relate to each other is a reflection of how we relate to God. We will love, honor, submit to, and be intimate with our spouses proportionately to how we love, honor, submit to, and are intimate with Jesus. In fact, most of the challenges we face in life are because we don't pursue God before our own needs. We don't deal with the "self-me-my-I" barrier, and therefore it blinds us to our shortcomings and becomes a stumbling block between ourselves and every commitment and relationship we have in life.

Husbands and wives who spend their lives expecting the other to fill their need for intimacy will forever be disappointed. Divorce, remarriage, or even living with another person will never meet that need for intimacy if you never address the heart of the problem. To meet our deep-seated need for peace, security, and companionship that only comes with an intimate relationship with your spouse, you will first have to find those things in your relationship with God. If you are not content in and at peace with God, then your spouse will never be able to fill that gap. What will fill the gap instead is more of self.

There are no quick fixes or communication exercises you can practice to transform your marriage if this heart issue is not first addressed. Learning how to better regulate your behavior or manage your conflicts does nothing in the end if there is no change of heart. When we counsel couples, we tell them the truth, and we tell it to them early in the process whether they are Christians or not. They must each take responsibility for their relationship with one another by first taking responsibility for their personal relationship with God. If they are to open the communication lines with their spouse, they have to first open their communication lines with God. If they want to get to know their spouse more intimately, they must open their hearts to God. The more they grow spiritually, the more they will grow in love with each other.

Most of the time we try to make our marriages better by working out our challenges with one another, rather than working on the challenges between ourselves and God. We each have a personal responsibility to love and serve God above everything else that we do in this life. Everything begins and ends with Jesus—and our willingness to pursue Him. James 4:8 says, *"Draw near to God and He will draw near to you."* His mercy and love will be upon us and work through us to the degree we are willing to open our lives and yield ourselves to Him. This is God's ultimate intention: intimacy. We wait and hope in God so that we can be enveloped by His tender mercy and loving-kindness.

God never intended for us to change each other in marriage, but for us to complete each other—so He could in turn change us individually.

When husbands and wives finally give up trying to change each other and allow God to change them instead, they will grow closer to each other. God never intended for us to change each other in marriage, but for us to complete each other—so He could in turn change us individually. I can't make that choice for you though—and you can't make that choice for each other. We can only make the choice in our own personal life to do what's right before God, to seek Him and serve Him and live for Him, and let the Holy Spirit of God take control of how we respond to our spouse. And, as you will find out in the next chapter, I haven't always done that. The wisdom I share here is hard won—so hard won, in fact, that except for the grace of God, Billie and I wouldn't still be married to one another sharing this message with you.

You may still be thinking, "Well, Mr. Counselor, you just don't understand how bad things are between my spouse and me. You've probably had it easy—what I am going through right now is worse than anything you have ever experienced." If you feel that way, then I urge you to read at least one more chapter before you set this book down.

I've heard it said that marriage is the closest to Heaven or hell we will ever get on this earth—but Billie and I know that sometimes you have to go through hell before you get a taste of the heaven on earth that marriage can be.

CHAPTER 7

FACING "FOR WORSE"

More marriages might survive if the partners realized that sometimes the better comes after the worse. —Doug Larson

𝒯hings truly did change for us that day in Victoria, Texas, when I gave my heart to Jesus and became a new man. My violent behavior and drinking fell away from me immediately. I know that at that point finding Jesus saved our marriage, and the vigor with which I had done wrong before was replaced with the hunger to be right before God. I read the Bible like I had never read any book before, was in church every time the doors were open, and was constantly listening to sermons or teachings on cassette whenever I could.

When God truly changes your heart, your life turns around in wonderful ways.

When God truly changes your heart, your life turns around in wonderful ways, but at the same time the "you" underneath it all—your nature that wants its own way, your life experience of hurts, pain, and struggles, and your needs for fulfillment, acceptance, recognition, and the like—is still there just as it was before. Your heart change means that your life is pointed in a new, much healthier direction in connection with the Spirit of God, but when your "self" still clings to the steering wheel of your life, sooner or later selfishness will steer you in the wrong direction if left unchecked.

As you may know from experience, being a Christian doesn't automatically make you a better person, but it is the "living day in and day out overcoming selfishness to be more like Jesus" that creates change. No matter how remarkably a person came to God, when he or she lets other things cloud their daily walk, it won't be long before they lose sight of where God is leading them and head off in the wrong direction once again. If there are no course corrections along this path, it is just as natural for a Christian to end up shipwrecked on a rocky shore as it is for anyone else.

Unfortunately, we see this happen all of the time to fellow Christians no matter how mighty or meek they once were. The reason is that no matter how much you *know* better, there are still choices to be made every day—you have to *choose* to live in love or give in to selfishness with each and every situation you face.

For we men especially, ego can blind us to the original nature of what we set out to do. When we feel those around us praising us and patting us on the back before we have the maturity to deal with it, it can easily go to our heads. This is why the Bible advises to let young Christians get their bearings and some experience in living for God before making them a teacher of others or giving them authority in the church. However, the week after I gave my life to Jesus, our pastor made me a Sunday school teacher, and regardless of the choices I was making in private, I felt that was an acknowledgment that I was living right before everyone else.

Such thought patterns can easily lead into living life legalistically, which leads to a dryness and deadness of spirit, exactly the opposite of living life from the heart led by God's Spirit and the voice of our conscience. Living like this begins an internal bartering with ourselves to justify whether or not we are "good" people. We subconsciously add up all the bad we don't do—"well, I have never murdered anyone, I stopped drinking, I don't beat my wife," etc., etc.—and then we add up the good we do—"I always attend church, they have even made me a teacher there, I am earning good money in my job to support my family, I give regularly to charitable causes," etc., etc.

Through this type of reasoning we determine we are better than most, and thus we slowly creep away from our relationship with God. Slowly, on the inside, we ignore the real voice of God speaking to our hearts and gradually give in to the little acts of selfishness that steer our lives in the wrong direction once more.

For about eight months after that day in May 1971 when God got hold of me, I really did make some great strides in improving my attitude and behavior. However, these improvements were based on what I understood to be the rules of righteousness and not on a revelation of the law of love. I became offended at something the pastor did that I didn't think was right, and stopped going to church for a bit.

Before I got too far however, God got hold of me again and released a new level of grace into my life. I was a businessman at that time, doing pretty well for our young, growing family, but I had been wrestling with God's call to the ministry. In a few months, I surrendered to that call.

Billie and I went into the ministry together as I started preaching in local churches and she would sing. Gradually I ministered farther and farther from home and she accompanied me less and less often. For the next eight years or so, really the rest of the 1970s, things were going well for us. We had three children, and we felt we were really living the life God had called us to live. God had opened great doors for our ministry and our schedule was full every year.

Growth or Stagnation?

Temptation still had a beachhead in my life however, and at the dawn of the 1980s, feeling I had "arrived" to some degree as a "man of God," I started giving into little things my selfish nature wanted. For one, I had never really given up my temper, something that made me more judgmental and critical as the years went on.

During this time, it was thought to have been something to survive a Paul Tsika revival. I could really roast people over a holy flame examining their lives under a microscope, while at the same time washing over some of those same things in my own life. Oddly, people benefitted from those sermons—God still used me to touch lives for the better—yet slowly but surely, I was growing prouder and more hard-of-heart to the very things I was preaching against. The more I failed on the inside, the more I tried to prove on the outside—through the conviction with which I preached—that I was right with God.

It was during the early 1980s that I really began to travel more. Great doors of opportunity had opened. I was preaching on national platforms with some of the most noted pastors of the day. More invitations to minister in churches and conferences were coming into our office than I could keep up with. Sometimes too much, too soon can give a man a false sense of where those blessings come from. God's Word is true, *"Pride goes before destruction and a haughty spirit before a fall"* (Prov. 16:18).

I was headed in that direction thinking I would be the exception and the rules didn't apply to me. I had regular messages I could preach by heart so I didn't need to do the work of studying for new ones, and my ministry was growing to the point I somewhat unconsciously felt I could give myself a break in some of the areas of my life where I had been so strict before.

It was a very subtle, very gradual drifting back toward old ways. I eased up on what I allowed myself to watch and began watching things in hotels I wouldn't have watched with Billie—not pornography, but things that bordered on arousing the wrong desires in me. I began to give in to my anger more, and some of the hurts and frustrations from my past that I had never really let God heal in me started to resurface.

Not needing to study so much, I drifted away from reading the Bible and praying as regularly as I had before, and slowly the ship of my life started to turn in ways to which I was blind. It wasn't that I didn't love God or my heart didn't still belong to Him, but I was slowly becoming lukewarm in my commitments, and that was slowly opening the door for my selfish "self-me-my-I" nature to have its way again.

Bitterness, anger, and frustration increasingly bubbled up in my life and Billie was often the focus of these emotions. I remember one time coming home from a speaking trip, tired and irritated, and Billie had made me a nice welcome home dinner, but had forgotten to get the Diet Coke, which I always had with my meals. I just lost it.

I ran my hands down the middle of the table, splattered food all over my family, knocked them out of their chairs, and then picked up the table and threw it against the wall putting a large hole where it hit. The kids were screaming and crying, but I didn't care. I knew I had damaged more than the wall that day. And although I was appalled with what I had done, I didn't go to God and repent, but grew even more self-obsessed and judgmental.

Not going up the marriage triangle to God to deal with my issues, I was instead building up the "self-me-my-I" barrier between Billie and me. I was slowly undermining what I actually wanted for our marriage. As a result, I was finding less and less fulfillment there and started giving in to the lie that I deserved to be treated better than I perceived I was being treated, even though Billie was being a wonderful wife and doing her best to take care of me and our family. I am sure she really didn't know what to do about the gulf she felt growing between us because of the way I was acting.

Some of us can go a lifetime slowly giving in to this kind of selfishness, undermining our closest relationships.

Some of us can go a lifetime slowly giving in to this kind of selfishness, undermining our relationships with those we are closest but never quite doing enough to completely break them off. Those people can live for decades unfulfilled on the inside, but looking good to everyone else on the outside. Others will let this eat at them to the point they just want to start over, scrap the relationship they have now, walk out on their families, or even change occupations in a desperate attempt to find what their heart is really looking for—whether they're looking for it in the right places or not.

Others try to cling to both worlds, but finally expose their inner corruption when temptation meets opportunity and they make a blunder that will either wake them up or cause them regret for the rest of their lives.

I fell into both categories.

While everything looked good on the outside to those around us, inside I had grown increasingly corrupt and selfish. I had rebuilt the barrier between Billie and me, and had hardened my heart toward God to the point that my desires to please myself were smothering my desires to please Him. Thus, in the mid-1980s, as a favor, I was counseling the daughter of a close friend whose marriage was on rocky ground and who was separated from her husband. I accept complete responsibility for the adultery that followed between us: my choice, my failure, and my becoming a stumbling block to another person. God would ultimately use this event to bring me to the end of my struggle and begin a new work in me.

When I say it was hell on earth, I only begin to express the regret I still have for what happened those decades ago. It was a devastating failure in my life that I have fought to keep others from going through ever since.

Weeks later, when my friend confronted me about the issue, I denied anything had ever happened. I left that meeting with him and told my family we should leave early for the next place I was supposed to preach. I had convinced Billie and the kids that this would be a great chance to spend some family time together, though the truth was I just wanted to get out of town. As that meeting came and went, I was falling apart on the inside. I was desperate for an answer. I knew I would either do something dreadfully crazy and destructive, or I had to come clean before everyone and confess.

So I sat down and wrote the most difficult letter of my life to my friend, telling him what had actually happened and throwing myself on his mercy. As I did so, I broke on the inside. I wanted to do whatever I could to make it right. When we returned to town, I went to his house to ask for forgiveness in person, but left with the issue still unresolved. He wanted to bury the issue because of our daughter's upcoming wedding. He loved our daughter and didn't want anyone or anything to be a cloud over her wedding day. We will forever be thankful to a gracious friend who considered our daughter's special day. So I left the area to speak in various places and avoided going back for some time.

For months I was unable to tell Billie or my family what had happened, but the issue came to a head later when I received one of the most heartbreaking letters of my life. A board had been formed to ask for my resignation as Staff Evangelist from the church. I did so knowing it would have been very difficult under the circumstances to be restored in that church. I truly came to the end of myself that day and knew I had to tell Billie what had happened.

I asked her to fly out to where I was preaching at that time and she was very excited to have a break from home and be with me on the road. When I picked her up at the airport, I was brokenhearted, knowing what I would be sharing with her later. After the service and fellowship that evening, we returned to the hotel. She was lying in bed and I knelt down beside her. My heart felt like melting wax as I confessed my infidelity to her and watched her whole countenance change. At first she said she didn't believe me, but as I continued she began to weep. I think I loved her more at that moment than I ever had. I asked her, "Billie, please don't leave me." Her reply was simply, "I don't want you to even think about that. By God's grace we will work through this." I cannot tell you what that meant to me at that moment. To have a faithful wife who loved me that much. That was a very long night for both of us.

The next day we toured around the town and found ourselves standing inside a beautiful chapel. A blank stare on both of our faces, we were still numb from the events of the night before. Words meant little and it was very difficult for Billie to look at me. I searched her face for any sign of forgiveness and all I saw was hurt. Her eyes were filled with the pain that I had put there. Yet I knew in my heart she loved me and was asking God for strength to walk through this valley.

That day some friends came to take us across the state to their church where my next meeting was. There was an awkward silence throughout the whole trip. Our friends knew something was wrong, but loved us enough not to inquire. The next day was Sunday. Billie was supposed to sing before I preached, but she couldn't. Our friends again didn't inquire—they just loved us.

I stood to preach, but my heart was broken over the grief I had caused my wife. The words came out and so did my sorrow. A Puritan once said, "If we could see sin five minutes before we commit it, like we see the consequences after, we would never sin." I couldn't go back and undo what I had done. I think I would have given my life to undo my violation to those I loved so much. That afternoon Billie boarded a plane for home. She told me not to worry, but that she needed a little time alone to think and pray. She had a layover where our daughter Gretchen lived at the time and they had a short visit in the airport. Billie didn't say a word to her about the events of the past few days. I know that had to have been the hardest trip she has ever taken.

Broken Hearts Together

As a wife, I suspected something was terribly wrong with Paul about this time, and somehow I knew on the inside what had probably happened, but I never really wanted to let myself admit consciously what I knew. It was too painful to believe. As all of this was unfolding, I wondered why our friends seemed so distant or why I wasn't asked to sing in our home church anymore.

So when Paul called me and asked me to fly out to be with him, I was excited because I was always thrilled when we got the chance to minister together. I got some strange looks though when I told others I was going, as they were in on what the board had decided while I was still living in denial about what I sensed in my heart.

That night when Paul told me what had happened, it was like getting hit in the face with a brick. I went through denial, anger, and grief all in a few moments. Yet, I also saw the remorse in his eyes, and though I had considered divorcing him on one occasion during his drinking binges early in our marriage when we'd lived in Maine, divorcing him never crossed my mind that evening.

I couldn't sleep at all that night. When dawn finally broke the next morning, it still felt as if the sun had never come up.

All the life in me was drained out and I had no idea how to face the future. I didn't want to talk, didn't know what to think, and didn't have any clue how to move forward. I felt completely lifeless. Paul was still speaking at a church there, and it was so tough because I didn't want to let people see that I was hurting, but at the same time, I knew I couldn't help it. It was like every face I saw was looking right through me and knew every dirty detail I had been in denial about all those weeks.

That night Paul and I sat down and I asked him every question that weighed on my heart. Paul was completely honest with me about everything I asked him. He would have told me anything I wanted to know, but I wasn't interested in the specific details of his indiscretion. I asked about how it had happened, why, how long it had been going on, and the things that concerned me most about his intentions for the future.

For my future peace of mind, I didn't want to have to wonder about any of these things ever again, because I knew how toxic it would be to my soul. I asked about every suspicion I had ever had, and as difficult as it was for both of us, we spent the time we needed to clear his heart and mine. By the time we were done with that conversation, I knew Paul was truly repentant. I could see God was doing a work in his heart, so I braced myself to allow God to work in mine. The next several months were painfully difficult as we began to work toward healing some of the wounds that had been opened in our lives.

It is hard to describe how difficult that time was, because everything you see in your life is now colored by the realization that your husband has been unfaithful, you are not where you hoped to be, and your world is not as secure as you once thought.

Waves of hurt still ripple through you like the aftershocks of an earthquake. As feelings of self-pity and doubt creep into your mind, your thoughts wander to things you remember and you are tempted to believe your husband did things he never did. You discover a new opportunity to crumble again with each new day. A war rages in your mind between peace and despair—the outcome of which will be determined by what you choose to focus on.

I knew that if I had let my mind go off into some of these dark areas, I would have been totally devastated. I had to ask God to keep my mind on the right things and not let my thoughts wander into the wrong places and dwell there, or else anxiety over what I was capable of imagining would have decimated me.

As I gave my mind over to God, every promise I had ever heard, sang in a song, or read in the Bible about God's faithfulness welled up within me. Thoughts that He would never leave me nor forsake me, that He would see me through any and every difficulty, and that He will be my shield and protection against any attack came to mind as I chose to think about His promises rather than the pain. For every thought of failure and regret and betrayal, God gave me a promise, and in the months to come, Paul and I began to recover and to heal.

Coming Back from the Brink

Second Corinthians 7:10 (ESV) says, *"For godly grief produces a repentance that leads to salvation without regret, whereas worldly grief produces death."* When I confessed my unfaithfulness to my friend I believe I felt a worldly guilt for what I was going to lose in regard to my reputation, my friendships, my family, and the love of my life, my wife. While I confessed in the hope of being forgiven and hopefully eventually reconciled with him, in the next six months I was also impressed by the deep realization of what David had experienced: that my real sin was against God, and that it was only by breaking through my selfishness and confessing to Him first and foremost that I would ever be reconciled with anyone else.

That revelation led to what I came to understand about the marriage triangle and true intimacy discussed in the previous chapter. Only when I came to God with my whole heart, determined to give my *self* fully to Him and let Him transform me—to put my "self" on the altar as Abraham had Isaac and offer it to God without reservation—only then would true healing come.

For godly grief produces a repentance that leads to salvation without regret, whereas worldly grief produces death.

As I came to godly sorrow before Jesus and started pursuing Him anew, this time it was without a guard over my inner selfish nature, and real change started to take place. My temper began to disappear. My wandering eye that led me to first watch things I shouldn't have been watching, and look at women in ways I shouldn't have been looking, stopped. My mind didn't wander where it shouldn't go anymore.

I began to confront past hurts and painful memories in my life that had before been stumbling blocks for me and sore spots between Billie and me. I began to deal with these things honestly, eliminating their power to cripple my mind. I began to treat and talk to Billie differently, not from a wounded place of insecurity and aggression, but from a place of confidence and love. These were all things I had come to realize before I told Billie what had happened with my friend's daughter, and it was that sorrow that had allowed her to forgive me. Had this not been so, things might have ended on the day I confessed to Billie.

In the coming weeks and months, we moved to a new state and told our children about what had happened. They were incredibly redemptive and forgiving, and their only real concern was whether or not we would stay together. Once they knew we were committed to working it through and staying together, they were incredibly supportive. I stepped down from the ministry for a time as Billie and I took a break and went to Bible school. During those years I had a friend who gave me a job as a janitor, and though it was a tough time financially, we experienced God's grace in healing and restoring our relationship.

God and Our Failures

The fact that God immediately came in to start transforming me and our marriage doesn't lessen the grief I still feel today over what I did. I think those are probably the tears God will wipe away in Heaven one day. For a long time I measured every thing by how far it was away from that failure. I remember thinking, "Well, that's six months," and then, "That's a year," and then marking the passing of two years, five years, and ten from when I gave in to temptation and violated my marriage covenant. If you're not careful, though, you can make the mistake of measuring everything in life by your failure rather than by the glorious things God is doing in your heart and life now. I have finally stopped measuring my life in terms of the time that has passed since that failure, and started celebrating my life in terms of the wonderful marriage I have today.

Why do we share all of this? Talking about my moral failure is certainly something I would rather not do, because it still hurts to think about it even after all these decades later. But if I don't share with you what led up to it and how we were able to emerge from it together, I feel I can't speak with any authority about how you can protect, strengthen, and heal your marriage and how to avoid—or recover from—going through something like what we did.

I want you to know that no matter what you're going through, what you've been through in the past, and no matter what your challenges are today, there is still an opportunity for recovery and reconciliation, if you are willing to allow God to work in your heart. There is no wound that God can't heal. There is no breach that He can't mend. There is no mountain that He can't see you over or river that He can't help you ford. If you are willing to seek Him first and let intimacy with Him heal you, then your marriage can become the heaven on earth it was intended to be.

I am not making excuses for what I did and take full responsibility for my wrong decisions, but I have seen time and again that hurting people hurt other people. The messes in my life I was refusing to give to God and let Him heal in me eventually festered to the point that my actions spilled over to hurt those I cared about most. The frustrations I was feeling on the inside I vented on my family by being unduly harsh and critical at home.

Even though I was preaching to others every week about how to let God into their lives and heal them, I wasn't willing to do it myself. I would weep and bawl trying to change myself with the power of my will, but that never had any lasting effect. What a man will not learn by principal and precept, he must then learn by experience. I had to be devastated before God could bring me to the end of myself to learn that healing through Him was the only answer.

As we were attending Bible school and recovering from this setback, we didn't know if there would be a future for our ministry. I have always believed that failure is something we do, not who we are; but failure in this case caused unanticipated devastation to my entire sphere of family and friends. There were suddenly a lot of people who didn't trust me anymore. On more than one occasion, people who knew about what had happened wrote letters ahead of us to places we were going and sullied our reputation before we were even able to introduce ourselves. Moral failure often leads to the death of a marriage because of added pressure caused by things like this, and more often than not, the death of a ministry.

Somehow, though, God saw fit to see us through it all. He has helped us make what we have learned available to others so they might avoid making the same mistakes, or else recover from having made similar ones.

So the reason we share all of this is because Billie and I believe that what we learned during those difficult years can prove to be invaluable to your marriage, your children, and your future. We discovered grace we had never known, how to find peace in the midst of any storm, and how God really does bring good out of evil. Biblical repentance and restoration are at the center of this process.

There are a lot of great techniques and ways to improve your communications skills that we will be sharing in the following chapters—they provide a sort of toolbox that you can use to build a better marriage—but *the heart of the problem is still the problem of the heart.* If you are not dealing with that, none of the rest of what we share with you will matter. God is the only heart surgeon I know who can do that kind of bypass-the-self heart surgery necessary to turn your life and marriage around. If you can't trust Him with your heart, you will never be able to trust your spouse with it, and that lack of trust will eventually undermine your relationship.

Our whole world turned upside down because of my choices, but after years of allowing God to dig deep into our hearts, we've come out on the other side of this darkness into the bright light of His grace. Our life and ministry from the late 1980s to the present have been quantum leaps beyond anything we could have ever hoped for. God truly does restore the years that the locust and palmerworm eat up. He doesn't just start you over; He restores (makes up for) those lost years of life and fruitlessness. God does not make you go back to the beginning and start over, because He knows that life is a continual journey. Instead, He makes up for those seemingly lost years with a more productive, fruitful, and meaningful life than you could have ever dreamed possible.

CHAPTER 8

BECAUSE OF THE HARDNESS
OF OUR HEARTS

---

*The worst reconciliation is better than the best
divorce.* —Miguel de Cervantes Saavedra

*A divorce is like an amputation: you survive it, but
there's less of you.* —Margaret Atwood

I want to begin this chapter with a caution. This caution
comes from a little phrase in Matthew 19:8. This phrase in itself
is at the center of everything we want to say about divorce. We
believe it expresses the root cause of all divorce as well as every
other self-made devastation in a person's life. Remove what this
phrase represents from your life and there would be joy unspeak-
able and full of glory. We have lived long enough to recognize the
symptoms described by this phrase at work in our life and in the

life of those we counsel. When these symptoms are not reversed, the results are always the same—*ruin*.

This phrase is *"Because of the hardness of your hearts"* (Matt. 19:8). Dear reader, this is the problem in every human disconnection without exception. Someone has a hard, unyielding, unrepentant heart. We really believe that 100 percent of the time if each spouse will look into the mirror of their own heart and be willing to let God change them, He will. This has to do with choice, not chance.

Why do we fight and argue? Why do we throw the divorce word around? Why do we insist on having our own way? Why do husbands not love their wives? Why do wives not honor their husbands? The answer is simply that someone has a hard, cold heart. We see our own selves as right, and our spouses as wrong. We hold fast to self instead of dying to self and behaving like Jesus would toward our spouses.

I asked a man a question in one of my counseling sessions. He was trying to change his wife and having very poor results. Surprise, surprise. I said to him, "Sir, do you believe if we could get Jesus to come back and live with your wife for six months that He could change her heart."

He quickly replied, "Of course!"

I took a long look at him until I knew he was uncomfortable with my stare, then I said, "I thought you said you were a Christian."

"I am," he responded.

Then I said, "If you're a Christian then Christ Himself lives in you. And if your wife's not living with Christ it's because you won't let her because of your unwillingness to let Him live *through* you." I let him know that he could not use the excuse that he's only human any more. Because once a person becomes a Christian they cease to be only human. Their body is now the temple of the Holy Spirit and a Holy God has taken up residence in them. *No more excuses.*

God wants to touch with our hands, walk with our feet, speak with our mouth, think with our mind, and love with our heart. He wants to *re-present* Himself through us because we are now representatives of Him. Imagine what your life would be like if you would do that—what the world would be like if we all did it!

This is not a book about divorce, but about getting married and staying married. Therefore I want to deal with the issues that cause hardness of the heart that can lead to divorce. Our firm belief is that when people allow Jesus to soften their hearts toward Him, then they will always make the choice of unconditional love, acceptance, and forgiveness toward others, especially their spouses—and love (God's love coming out of us) *never* fails.

I know that there are biblical grounds for divorce. But a reversal of "hardness of the heart" would empower most couples for reconciliation. We also realize there are things beyond our understanding, and we don't pretend to have all the answers. There are issues of moral impurity, abandonment, abuse of all kinds, plus individual heartaches too numerous to mention. Billie and I never want to be cavilier about the grief that people go through nor take for granted God's grace in our own marriage.

This is why we wanted you to hear our story before we weighed in on this topic—so you would understand why we believe the way we do about divorce—and why we think reconciliation in a marriage is a much greater possibility than most couples believe today. Looking at the Scriptures, our own experiences, and into the lives of the hundreds of couples we have counseled, it is our belief that by God's grace and your cooperation, your marriage can be saved.

What if You've Already Been Divorced?

When the marriage covenant has been broken and the divorce papers have been finalized, the covenant obligation is, in fact, dissolved. When that happens there must be the freedom to marry another. One must be careful, however, because you are the same person who had trouble in your first marriage relationship and will certainly need to face the very same challenges in any new relationship.

If you don't do something about the issues you had in your previous marriage, odds are you will be right back in the same situation even faster than you were before. It is up to you whether you go through all of the same problems again, or you truly start over and do marriage better the second time. Remember, the *you* you see is the *you* you'll be.

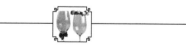

Remember, the you you see is the you you'll be.

But let me hasten to say that while divorce can be devastating, it is not the unpardonable sin. Many innocent people, after divorce, have gone on to find a wonderful life with a new spouse: one that honors God and is a blessing to others. And even if they are the most guilty partner in a divorce, there can be forgiveness and a life of no condemnation when there is true repentance. There are always consequences to our actions, but when there is a heart to do right, even after failure, you will find God's grace sufficient.

While I very much oppose divorce, at the same time I don't believe God wants people locked into destructive relationships either, especially destructive marriages. That's why godly counsel is so important. I think such decisions need serious consideration and solid, wise counsel before being acted upon. You can't make such weighty decisions in a vacuum.

Sometimes, though rarely, couples are better to separate for a time and then come back together to see if they are able to work things through. But, again, the decision to do this should only be carried out under reliable supervision. Sometimes we need a sane voice outside of our own to know what is right. For this reason, God has appointed pastors and counselors to intervene when we need it. It is very often the first step toward healing. I wish Billie and I had been privileged to receive such counsel when we were going through the process of putting our lives back together again. Struggling with disconnection and isolation as a couple only added to our already difficult and painful path to restoration.

Divorce's Injustice

While we already discussed the changes that happened in the United States since no-fault divorce was introduced into our society, we think the subject is worth looking at again in light of what the Bible has to say about divorce. Billie and I both believe that the way divorce procedures are set up today gives room for a great deal of abuse by unrepentant spouses. Because of no-fault divorce, innocent spouses bear the same penalty as unfaithful spouses and are often left without reasonable livelihoods when their spouse moves on.

Too often we've seen husbands with stay-at-home wives have repeated affairs and then decide to leave, splitting the house 50-50 with no obligation to pay alimony—yet moving on with their successful careers while their wives are left struggling to enter the workforce late in life. The abandonment, abuse, or adultery of a spouse is not considered when determining custody of the children or the final divorce settlement. In other instances, one partner breaks up the marriage for differences that could have been worked through, only to take their hang-ups into another marriage and wreak havoc there as well.

While going back to a system that demands that some fault be proven before divorces are legalized is unlikely, states should look at reforming the laws that govern getting divorced to make them more common-sensed and fair. In his article, "The Evolution of Divorce," Director of the National Marriage Project, W. Bradford Wilcox, advocates that states institute a one-year waiting period before a divorce can be filed and then combine that with a program that teaches the couples about the social and emotion consequences of divorce on their children.

Divorce courts should also be able to consider the conduct of the spouses in making decisions about alimony, property division, and child support and custody. Spouses divorced against their will who have not committed adultery, abused their children or spouse, or have not abandoned their family, should get preferential treatment by the courts. If such measures do not discourage divorce, they should at least institute a greater degree of justice in divorce cases and make couples think twice before using divorce as a legal means of abandoning their families with few repercussions.

Spouses divorced against their will who have not committed adultery, abused their children or spouse, or have not abandoned their family, should get preferential treatment by the courts.

Congress should also extend the federally funded Healthy Marriage Initiative that was started in 2006 as part of President George W. Bush's initiative to strengthen marriages and families among the poorest sectors of our nation. Many of these programs will be in the process of being evaluated for continued funding about the time this book is published—but if Congress does not allocate more funds to the initiative, then it won't matter how successful they have been. In the past we have also seen public initiatives to create marketing campaigns to do everything from getting people to stop smoking to encourage reading to keeping kids off drugs. Similar campaigns should be considered to encourage couples to get the help they need to stay married for the sake of their families and communities.

Our churches should also step up to address the issues of strengthening the quality and stability of marriages in their communities, both among their members and their neighbors. As a culture, we must change the way we view the institution of marriage as a convenience for mutual self-gratification to the important social foundational component that it is. Parents, schools, local governments, and school districts, and even the entertainment industry need to take a closer look at the way we value marriage and how we portray it to our children and society.

Recent research has shown that divorce and single-parent homes contribute more to poverty than unemployment or even a low minimum wage. Families that stick together make it through hardships much better than those that don't. However, if we are genuinely concerned with not passing the "sins of the fathers" on to future generations, as well as adding stability to our nation from the poorest families on up, then we must take a more serious look at how we view marriage and divorce. We must work harder to reduce the divorce rate so we can increase the number of children raised by two parents rather than just one.

As Bradford Wilcox puts it, "The unthinkable alternative is a nation divided more and more by class and marital status, and children doubly disadvantaged by poverty and single parenthood. Surely no one believes that such a state of affairs is in the national interest."[1] We are not only in agreement with Dr. Wilcox's conclusions, we are praying they will find favor at the grassroots of our nation.

Endnote

1. Bradford Wilcox, *The Evolution of Divorce.*

CHAPTER 9

FORBEARANCE EQUALS "FOR BETTER"

A happy marriage is the union of two good forgivers.
—Ruth Bell Graham

People talk about dreaming big—like they want a big car, a big house, a nice place on the lake, a wonderful career doing something meaningful for the world—but do you know what people *really* want? They want great relationships. God has designed us to want quality relationships, and family is always the foundation of every relationship in a person's life. When people see a great relationship between a husband and wife or between parents and their children, they know instinctively that's what they want most out of life. They want a relationship with their spouse and their kids and their grandkids that brings them fulfillment and a lifetime of love.

When Paul and I talk to people about their marriage relationship, we discuss it as if it were the most important thing on this earth—because it is. We *all* want to experience the level of trust, companionship, and intimacy that comes from a healthy marriage. Nobody wants to feel physically rejected by—or emotionally disconnected from—his or her spouse. There are very few people who desire to live a life of solitude, without family of any kind, alone with only God and nature. Who would want to be alone all of the time? Happiness is only real when it is shared, and best when it is shared with someone you love.

Happiness is only real when it is shared, and best when it is shared with someone you love.

That's why we're always so amazed to meet couples who start out so desperately in love, only to run into them a year—or five or ten years—later and learn they can no longer get along with each other. They come to us telling us they are planning to get a divorce, that they don't know why they ever married in the first place, and then launch into a list of their spouse's faults that they evidently have been compiling for several years. We ask ourselves, "Where did those two love birds go who were so determined and confident they would live happily ever after?"

In talking with these couples, we normally discover it is never really any one thing that has pushed them over the edge with each other. It is a string of little things—little slights, little side comments that dig at the other person's abilities or character, little annoying habits that are never dealt with, small thoughtless actions that rub each other the wrong way, one little forgotten promise after another—that slowly build up, one brick of separation at a time, until there is a huge wall between the two that neither of them remember building, and neither of them want to take responsibility for allowing to form.

Then, as they list each other's faults, we hear the "Well, he *always*…" or "You know, she *never*…" statements. We have tried to eliminate those two words from our conversations. Nobody *always* does something and it is never *never*. Using those two words creates frustration and helplessness. What's the use of ever trying if it really is something the other *always* or *never* does? These little annoyances with each other are expressed in sweeping generalities that have little to do with reality.

Slowly over time, one little thing after another has not been dealt with or resolved, and before they know it, they are two people living in the same house but in two completely different worlds. Something resembling the Great Wall of China has been erected out of all those little pebbles right down the middle of their relationship. The Song of Solomon describes it as *"the little foxes that spoil the vineyards"* (Song of Sol. 2:15 ESV).

While this wall is often what leads to thoughts of divorce, couples will also stay together no matter how distant and estranged they've become. Sometimes they don't even sleep in the same bed, but act as if that is quite normal for a married couple.

They have 20 or 30 years of unresolved issues between them for which they are unwilling to forgive one another. They have 20 or 30 years of unfulfilled IOUs to each other, and end up growing old before their time because of holding on to grudges that color everything that they do.

It's Time for the Wall to Come Down!

If a marriage relationship is going to succeed, husbands and wives must rip up their IOUs on a regular basis. You can't let your unfulfilled promises to each other stack up, or collect your spouse's mistakes like a list of criminal activities you hope to some day use against them in a court of law. The only way to do that is to have open and honest communications that deal with these issues while they are still "little foxes"—talk them through to resolution, and then *forgive* each other so that you can move on *together*.

For as much as the word *forgiveness* is thrown around in our culture, I think it is poorly understood. Too many confuse forgiveness with other things. For example, forgiveness is not tolerance—it is not overlooking a slight or a hurt and trying to forget it ever happened. It's not pretending something didn't happen, either. It's not generosity of spirit. I have seen people with generous spirits hold grudges right up there with the best of them. Forgiveness is not turning the other cheek or looking the other way. It's not trying to cover something up with your sense of humor by making a joke out of it. It's not politeness or tactfulness, and it's not being diplomatic.

All of these are attempts to cover up or brush aside an offense, but in the end, all that is accomplished is that the wrong is swept under the rug to be dealt with later on—where it grows like a neglected dust bunny—and when the rug is finally lifted, a matted collection of miscellaneous hurts have gathered that would choke any vacuum cleaner!

So what is forgiveness? Forgiveness is *a full pardon for the one who has done harm to you.* It's not something that you can do casually, because it is a *deliberate act of the will.* You have to make a conscious choice to forgive, just as you have to make a conscious choice to rejoice in the face of troubling circumstances or bad news.

Forgiveness means that you fully release the offender from his or her debt. It means fully clearing that person's record. It is a promise never, ever to bring up the offense against that person again to God, to others, or to the offender. Forgiveness is a willingness to accept the consequences of someone else's action without ever retaliating.

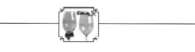

Forgiveness is a willingness to accept the consequences of someone else's action without ever retaliating.

Some may say, "Well, forgiveness seems too easy. There should be blood for blood and eye for eye. They shouldn't be able to get off without any repercussions!" You can require tooth for tooth in retaliation in some situations, but what repayment can you demand from a man who has broken your home or betrayed your children? What kind of payment can an unfaithful wife make to even things out with her husband? What can you ask from someone who has broken your heart? So few transgressions can be compensated for—and so seldom does the victim possess the power to demand recompense anyway. In most cases, making things right is beyond possibility. Repayment is impossible.

Forgiveness is really the only viable option without letting the hurt go on and on and on. But you say someone has to pay. You're right, but Someone did. Two thousand years ago Jesus died for us and because of us. He paid the debt so that we could forgive. Freely we have received forgiveness and freely we are to give it.

What about revenge? Why not get revenge on the person who wronged you? Well, your heart may say, "I want equal payment or restitution from the offender so they will at least know how they made me feel. I want to pay them back." We want to see people pay when they've hurt us. We want to even the score. You know that old saying, "Tit for tat, butter for fat, you kill my dog, I'll kill your cat"? But what will that really do for you? Will it really help you get free from the hurt they caused you?

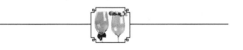

Holding on to a grudge is an acid that does more damage in the vessel in which it's stored than to the victim on which it's poured.

The truth is, it won't. You are still harboring a grudge, and that grudge will hurt you more than anything you can do to the other person. Holding on to that offense will only make you more bitter and angry as time goes by. Things that used to be small will suddenly be like the straw that broke the camel's back—even the smallest slight will start to push you over the edge. Holding on to a grudge is an acid that does more damage in the vessel in which it's stored than to the victim on which it's poured.

You may have heard the saying, "Unforgiveness is like drinking poison and thinking the one who offended you will die from it." I believe that is true. Unforgiveness is *your* weight to bear, and the person you aren't forgiving may never even know you were wronged by what they did in the first place! Unforgiveness is locking yourself in a prison and then pretending like the one who offended you has the key—as if it were up to them to do something about the situation in which you have trapped yourself. However, it is up to you alone whether you stay in that jail cell or walk free. Forgiveness is your key to freedom.

Forgiveness is your key to freedom.

What Are You Allowing to Fester?

It is possible to carry around bitterness and unforgiveness and not fully recognize it because you have buried it so deeply. It could be something from your childhood or a past relationship, but it is still eating at you and may even be coming between you and your spouse without you realizing it. Stop and ask yourself the following questions and see how they affect you. Do you find any of these statements to be true? (Just fill in the blanks with the first name that pops into your head.)

- Every time I think of _____, I still feel angry.

- I have a subtle secret desire to see _____ pay for what they did to me.

- Deep in my heart I wouldn't mind if something bad happened to_____.

- I sometimes find myself telling others how _____ hurt me.

- If _____'s name comes up, I am more likely to say something negative about him/her than something positive.

If you find any of these to be true, then you still have unforgiveness in your heart toward the person or people whose names you used to fill the blanks. Or, you may have tried to forgive that person at one point, but then took the offense back later because you couldn't keep from dwelling on it again.

There also may be something that happened in your life that you feel gives you the right to be unforgiving—something that was more than just a slight or hurt feeling. It could be that:

- you've been lied to.

- important promises were broken.

- you've been neglected by your parents or by your grown children.

- you've experienced a violent crime against self or someone you loved.

- you've been treated unfairly by an employer.

- your parents divorced when you were young.

- you were robbed.

- you were slandered or falsely accused of something that cost you dearly.

- your spouse committed adultery or divorced you unfairly.

- you were cheated in a business or financial deal.

- you have a rebellious or wayward son or daughter.

- your parent or mate abused alcohol and/or drugs.

- you were abandoned by a parent or mate.

- you were publicly humiliated, belittled, rejected.

- you were abused physically, emotionally, or sexually.

Do any of these experiences strike home? If they do, then you need to forgive again, and leave the offense on the altar before God once and for all, refusing to entertain the thought when it comes up.

Only God has the ability to forget. He says, *"their sins and their iniquities will I remember no more"* (Heb. 8:12 KJV). God can choose not to remember. We can't do that, but what we can do by His grace is choose not to allow that thought to lodge in our hearts. When any issue of unforgiveness comes up, we can choose to say, "I have forgiven and I choose to continue to forgive." As we adopt this strategy, the voice of unforgiveness will grow quieter and quieter.

Deciding to Forgive Is Just the First Step

Just because you have forgiven someone doesn't mean the offense will never hurt again. You may have forgiven and still be struggling with painful feelings and memories.

I've heard people say that, "Forgiveness is easy. It's no big thing." But that's not true when we've been deeply hurt, especially in a marriage when we've made ourselves vulnerable to each other. Intimacy requires vulnerability, yet the more vulnerable we allow ourselves to be, the more deeply we will feel the pain of disappointment. When you have been hurt on this deep of a level, the decision to forgive is only the starting place. It can be like a winding road that requires you to pay attention in order to stay on it. Although forgiveness is an immediate decision, it may take awhile for the feelings of hurt to heal.

Much like a wound goes through a healing process, so does a breach in a relationship. Restoration, like healing, requires time and patience. The initial act of forgiveness is like stitching up a wound—but the healing isn't complete until new cells grow to take the place of the stitches. Just as new growth must replace what was lost, forgiveness must be followed by a positive investment in the relationship. The redemptive power of forgiveness is not complete until there is total restoration—until the severed relationship is wholly mended.

The new weld of forgiveness should afterward result in a deeper, stronger union than existed before. People think they can say, "I forgave him (or her), but I don't want to have anything to do with him (or her) ever again. As far as I am concerned, he (she) is dead." But that is not forgiveness. The final step in forgiving is to do something to heal the wound until nothing remains but the forgotten scar. You have to put feet to what you say. Forgiveness is acceptance with no exceptions. It accepts not only the hurt you've received, but it also accepts the one who did the hurting—and it accepts the losses caused by the hurtful actions or words. This is not something you can do with normal, human love, though—it takes the *agape* love of God.

The final step in forgiving is to do something to heal the wound until nothing remains but the forgotten scar.

Forgiveness is the key to your recovery to wholeness. As Jesus says in Luke 6:27-31 (ESV):

> *But I say to you who hear, "Love your enemies, do good to those who hate you, bless those who curse you, pray for those who abuse you. To one who strikes you on the cheek, offer the other also, and from one who takes away your cloak do not withhold your tunic either. Give to everyone who begs from you, and from one who takes away your goods do not demand them back. And as you wish that others would do to you, do so to them"* (Luke 6:27-31 ESV)

Jesus was not telling this to people because of the social impact it would have, but for the sake of those *"who hear."* It is the Golden Rule: *"As you wish that others would do to you, do so to them."* It is the path to reclaiming your own joy and peace.

There is really nowhere that forgiveness is more important than in marriage.

There is really nowhere that forgiveness is more important than in marriage. If you don't choose to forgive your spouse, then every little thing that happens can create an uncomfortable friction between you. After all, you cannot *earn* forgiveness, so if you don't *choose* to forgive, the best that can happen is a slow erosion of your intimacy. You have to focus your mind on the restoration and refuse to give past offenses another thought, otherwise your marriage will—at best—become something you endure rather than truly enjoy.

The Battlefield of the Mind

Over the years as Paul and I have counseled couples, we've found that, very often, what we all need most is to stop *listening* to ourselves and to start *speaking* to ourselves. We shouldn't be the victims of our thoughts and memories, but too often we are. We choose not to control the thoughts running around in our heads, so when something reminds us of a past hurt, it's as if we are reliving it all over again.

However, disciplined thinkers will use their thoughts to build better futures for their loved ones and themselves. It all starts with what we think and what we tell ourselves. Philippians 4:8 (ESV) puts it this way, *"Whatever is true, whatever is honorable, whatever is just, whatever is pure, whatever is lovely, whatever is commendable, if there is any excellence, if there is anything worthy of praise, think about these things."*

These are the things we need to speak to ourselves. Ephesians 5:19 (KJV) says, *"Speaking to yourselves in psalms and hymns and spiritual songs, singing and making melody in your heart to the Lord."* Not only are we to think on things above, but we are also to speak those things.

What we all need most is to stop listening to ourselves and to start speaking to ourselves.

Even after I had forgiven Paul for all that had happened between us, I still knew there were certain places I couldn't let my mind go. For a long time, it didn't take much for some incident to trigger a memory that would bring all the hurt and insecurities flooding back over me again. But as I once heard a preacher say, "While you can't keep a bird from flying over your head, you don't have to let it build a nest in your hair!" Thoughts and feelings will come, but that is when you need to turn your thoughts around by speaking to yourself about what is true, honorable, just, pure, lovely, commendable, excellent, and worthy of praise in order to shoo those bad memories away.

You have to speak to yourself and say, "I forgave that. It may still hurt, but those things are in the past and we are putting things back together now. These are the things I love about my spouse, and these are the things we are planning together. I am going to think on the good things about our being together and nail the rest of it to the cross of Jesus. It is forgiven just as Jesus has forgiven me."

While you can't keep a bird from flying over your head, you don't have to let it build a nest in your hair!

Memorize Scriptures you find comforting and repeat them to yourself whenever the wrong thoughts come along. Remind yourself constantly of God's promises to see you through. It may take awhile, but eventually you will find your thoughts *and* circumstances turning in the right direction. Things will begin to change for the better and when you look in the rear-view mirror remembering what happened, it will no longer carry with it the same devastating feelings, but appear more and more as the tough life lesson it actually was.

What you fill your mind with is what you become. Proverbs 23:7 states, *"For as he thinks in his heart, so is he."* You reap in your life what you sow in your mind. Garbage in, garbage out. Right things in, right things out. It's a law of the mind that God created so that we could steer our destinies. If you fill your mind with loving thoughts, then you're going to have a greater tendency to walk in love. If you focus your thoughts on all the wrongs, you will most likely walk in resentment and bitterness.

When you squeeze a lemon, what comes out of it? Most people will say lemon juice. Well that's likely, but the fact is you could take a syringe, extract the lemon juice from it, and inject orange juice into the lemon. If you did that, when you squeezed the lemon, what would come out? Orange juice. In other words, no matter what something looks like on the outside, when you squeeze it, you will get out whatever it is filled with.

A lot of people look sweet and lovely on the outside, but when they are squeezed by a tough situation, what happens? Out comes bitterness, anger, contempt, or hatred expressed in a string of expletives. Everything is about them, what happened to them, what was done to them, and how the people who did that have destroyed their hopes and dreams—or, basically, out comes the result of years and years of unforgiveness. Though we may be handsome or beautiful on the outside, what we think about most of the time determines what we are like on the inside. If we forgive, we are free to be who we want to be—if we don't, we are taken captive by the bitterness, anger, and insecurities of being wronged.

The Bible likens bitterness to a root that once planted digs deeply into our souls, spreading its influence and flavoring every aspect of our lives. The seed that sprouts into a root of bitterness is offense. When we experience an offense, we have the choice to do one or two things. We can immediately snatch that seed up and toss it away, or we can cultivate it. We can water it. We can constantly think about it and give it our energy. Then slowly, invisibly, like a root under the soil, it will spread and grow and become harder and harder to get out of our lives.

Hebrews 12:15 (ESV) says, *"See to it that…no 'root of bitterness' springs up and causes trouble, and by it many become defiled."* That's what happens with bitterness and unforgiveness. It defiles everything. It defiles how you speak to others. It defiles your marriage relationship. It defiles your friendships. It defiles your business. It will defile every aspect and arena of your life. It will even make you physically sick.

Bitterness is a result of dwelling too long on a hurt. It's the result of not forgiving an offender. Because of the stress it causes, we suffer from dis-*ease* (disease). Our families are destroyed, and the next generation is even poisoned as we pass our unforgiving attitudes on to our children. When we don't forgive, everybody around us suffers. So when that little hurt comes, don't dwell on it. Forgive and move on, filling your mind with what you want—not what you don't want. Believe it or not, it is a choice, and it is *your* choice.

When we don't forgive, everybody around us suffers.

The Appreciation Principle

You choose your attitude. You can choose love and forgiveness or strife and bitterness. The law of love demands that we choose to show respect by honoring one another rather than undermining and complaining about each other. We must bring what we think and say into alignment with what we want and into alignment with what is true, pure, and virtuous. We must choose thoughts of peace and contentment—words of love and respect—over words of contempt and spite. We choose to be grateful for all that we have, to count our blessings, and to sow seeds of the good things we want to see grown in our lives—or we foolishly choose the bad things we don't want growing in our lives. There really isn't a middle ground.

As women, I think the main reason for our discontentment and inability to accept our husband is unrealistic expectations. I have heard it said that men get married hoping their wives will never change, while women get married with a list of changes they plan for their husband to make in the next few months! But as Paul has already said, we can never hope to change our spouses, we can only change ourselves. We will never be content until we stop setting goals that our spouses can never achieve.

We will never be content until we stop setting goals that our spouses can never achieve.

As wives, we must stop expecting our husbands to be someone they are not. A man must be able to prayerfully set the goals God gives him with the loving support of his wife, otherwise all that will come to the marriage is division and strife. Sometimes it takes great trust in God to have a little faith in our husbands. We must respect our husbands as the man God created him to be. It is one of the basic needs of a man to be respected by his wife, and that is *our* choice. It is not up to the husband to command—or demand—the respect of his wife, just as it is not up to the wife to demand the love of her husband. Respect, like love, is a choice.

When I counsel young women I hear all kinds of crazy things about their husbands. Sometimes I want to tell her to just go ahead and shoot him, but I know better, because the husband, just like the wife, is a work of God in progress. Instead I will remind her that just as love is a choice, so is respect—and until she chooses to respect him for who God is making him to be, she is not allowing God to change him.

Remember, there is a difference between expectations *for* someone and *of* someone. When we have expectations *of* someone, it means we have a bar raised in our minds that we expect them to live up to. When they don't reach it, there is a built-in punishment of some kind. We ignore or we don't acknowledge them in some significant way. We know they are insecure, so that's our way of manipulating and trying to control them.

But when we have expectations *for* someone, it means the bar is not raised. Therefore we leave that person to the Lord. We cooperate with Him by being proactive in praying for, encouraging, and edifying the person. This doesn't mean you are indifferent to his or her growth either. What we are simply doing is acknowledging that all of our efforts to change the person have only left us frustrated.

We need to not only accept our husband as he is—having expectations *for* him—but demonstrate gratitude for all that our husband has done and is doing for us. A man is attracted to a grateful woman. Nothing is worse than a woman who is always discontented and never satisfied. We must give our expectations to God, and accept with joy what He gives us in return. Expectations will weigh us down and squeeze the life out of our marriages if they are not from God.

Remember that the marriage covenant is an agreement to yield our rights and accept our responsibilities. That is for both the husband *and* the wife. In other words, we have areas where God needs to work on us, and there are areas that God wants to work on your husband. Let Him—don't take him out of God's hands by trying to manipulate and mold him yourself. Or a wife may be expecting her husband to fulfill a need only God can meet, and that can only lead to disappointment.

We each need to have a fulfilling relationship with God on our own if we ever really want to have intimacy with each other. A wife may anticipate that her needs should be met on her terms and time schedule rather than according to God's will, but we have to let those things go and let God be God. We can demonstrate gratefulness by learning to be content in our relationship with God first, and that attitude will then spread to our husbands and throughout our homes. After all, *"True godliness with contentment is itself great wealth"* (1 Tim. 6:6 NLT).

CHAPTER 10

How to Fight Fair

*All married couples should learn the art of battle as
they should learn the art of making love. Good battle
is objective and honest—never vicious or cruel. Good
battle is healthy and constructive, and brings to a
marriage the principle of equal partnership.*
—Ann Landers

*F*alling in love and getting married is relatively easy compared to building a good marriage. Once the honeymoon is over, we learn the layers of self that were peeled away, as we fell in love, are relatively shallow compared to the layers that need to go in order to have true intimacy. Sometimes that level of intimacy isn't achieved until several years, even decades, into the marriage—and sometimes it is never achieved. It depends on the work we each allow God to do in our hearts.

As Billie and I have already shared, we were married more than a decade and had three school-aged children before real heart issues came into question because of my moral failure. Most people don't experience something as earth shattering as we did, although they still have to face the same issues with self-centeredness. While it is a painful process to strip away self so that our hearts can be fully shared with one another, marriage will never be all it can be without it.

We truly believe that God created marriage so that we would have someone to complete us. There are no two more important relationships on the earth than with God and with your spouse. When we come to Christ, we are returned to spiritual wholeness—we are born anew in our spirit so we can have fellowship with God who is Spirit. Marriage, on the other hand, is intended to make us one. The wife is meant to complete the husband, and the husband to complete the wife. There are things the wife will see in her husband that the husband is blind to himself; and there are things the husband will see in his wife that she will never see by herself. We all have "rough edges" that need to be smoothed so that we can become mature adults contributing to our work, churches, friends, family, and society. These rough edges are worn smooth either through conversation or conflict—either by gentle sandpaper or a jagged-toothed file.

God uses marriage to perfect us. Issues surrounding our imperfections should be dealt with through constructive dialogs between husbands and wives, yet too often these attempts turn into destructive conflicts—fights void of mercy that erect barriers instead of tender conversations that build walls of protection. It is only when honest and open conversations happen on a regular basis that a couple is protected against whatever comes against them.

It is only when honest and open conversations happen on a regular basis that a couple is protected against whatever comes against them.

I heard a story some time ago (back when there used to be gas station attendants who would clean your windshields as well as fill your tank with gas!) that I think illustrates this point beautifully:

A man, with his wife, drives into a gas station. The windshield is dirty and the husband asks the attendant to wash it. The attendant washes it and the husband says, "It's still dirty. Do it again." So the attendant attacks it again. The husband looks at it squinting, only to exclaim, "Man, it's still dirty!" and begins to get really upset with the attendant. "I'm going to talk with your boss and have you fired! The thing is still dirty! Don't you know how to do your job?"

About that time, his wife reaches over and removes his glasses, carefully wipes them with a tissue, and puts them back on his face. The driver, embarrassed, slumps into the seat as he observes a spotless windshield.

We all have lenses that we see the world through, and sometimes they need cleaning or adjusting. But where do we find the perspective outside of our own that we can trust enough to help us see more clearly?

Certainly this change of perspective can come through something we read, someone at work, a friend, or even a child, but it should most often come through honest conversations with the ones who know and love us best—our spouses. As the safeguards of our hearts, our spouses should be the first ones to help us get the "logs" out of our own eyes that make us so critical of the "specks" we see in the lifestyles of others (see Matt. 7:3-5). Our spouses should be the ones working with us on our deepest heart issues to help us become who God has called us to be.

Yet this level of communication and trust is also the most difficult to develop. Trying to reach the heart of our spouse in this way is like trying to break into a high-security facility with layers of alarms, traps, and defenses that have been constructed to keep anyone from getting in.

The fact is, we can never break into another's heart—we can only disarm our own heart allowing the other in. That takes conscious, committed persistence, because quite often we don't even know how many defenses we have put up over the years. Too often, as we begin to let the other one in, it is only to have them trigger some trap we weren't even aware was there. We strike out in self-defense and leave them running away wounded as a result. Or the opposite may happen. Either way, we have a choice to make— we can pull away or try again to let each other in.

Buttons, Buttons, Who's Pushing Buttons?

Everyone knows the old saying, "Sticks and stones may break my bones, but words will never hurt me." Well, whoever made that up has never been married! The saying should really go, "Sticks and stones may break my bones, but words can squeeze the very heartbeat from my chest, the very breath from my soul, the lift from my walk, the twinkle from my eyes, and the hope from my day. Please throw sticks and stones! At least broken bones will heal!"

Proverbs 21:19 (ESV) puts it this way, *"It is better to live in a desert land, than with a quarrelsome and fretful woman."* And Proverbs 27:15 (ESV) says, *"A continual dripping on a rainy day and a quarrelsome wife are alike."* Had Solomon handed his pen to one of his wives, imagine what she might have said about belittling husbands! The truth is, words do hurt, and their effects are long lasting. As Billie shared in the last chapter, it may seem easy to forgive what your spouse says to you, but it takes real effort to truly get the hurt of it out of your life.

Or perhaps we should be more careful about what we say to each other in the first place. The Bible has a lot to say about the power of our tongues to wound one another. According to James 3:2-6 and verse 10:

> *For we all stumble in many things. If anyone does not stumble in word, he is a perfect man, able also to bridle the whole body. Indeed, we put bits in horses' mouths that they may obey us, and we turn their whole body. Look also at ships: although they are so large and are driven by fierce winds, they are turned by a very small rudder wherever the pilot desires. Even so the **tongue** is a little member and boasts great things. See how great a forest a little fire kindles! And the tongue is a fire, a world of iniquity. The tongue is so set among our members that it defiles the whole body, and sets on fire the course of nature; and it is set on fire by hell. ... Out of*

the same mouth proceed blessing and cursing. My brethren, these things ought not to be so. (James 3:2-6, 10)

The tongue has the power to direct and it has the power to sting like a whip. As a bridle turns a horse and a rudder steers a ship, the tongue will direct the nature and course of your relationships. The tongue has the power to destroy and the power to delight.

Remember when Billie asked you, "If you squeeze a lemon, what comes out?" Whatever is inside of it, right? Well, the place from where "whatever is inside of you" comes out is your mouth— and what comes out are the words you speak. If you are full of bitterness and past hurts, when you are squeezed a little in your relationship, out will come words of bitterness and hurt meant to strike and cut the other person to the core. You don't even have to think about it! In fact, you may not even realize it, but out of your mouth will spew poisonous words meant to assassinate the character of the other. Is it possible that from the same mouth will come both blessings *and* curses? Well, yes, that is possible, but *"these things ought not to be so."*

The tongue has the power to destroy and the power to delight.

If we are to have true intimacy with our spouses, we have to first do some housecleaning in our own souls so that we get rid of the junk in our lives and leave it at the foot of the cross of Jesus. We ask for forgiveness and we forgive—those past hurts and offenses have no further hold over us. Then we need to stir up thoughts of good toward our mates. It is one thing to eliminate the bad, but if we don't fill it with something good, we still won't be a blessing to our spouse when situations squeeze us.

We need to go beyond mutual respect to actually having goodwill toward each other. That is where *agape* love comes in. No matter what comes against you, together you have to be determined that you are on the same side, and that you will support each other no matter what.

If you are not having regular, open, honest communications, however, you will not have this kind of support for each other. You will compete with your mate rather than completing him or her. You will make little comments trying to get your spouse to feel as neglected as you feel. You will push his or her buttons to try to get a reaction rather than speaking kindly. When you do these things, strife and confusion fill your home.

Ephesians 4:29 (ESV) advises, *"Let no corrupting talk come out of your mouths, but only such as is good for building up, as fits the occasion, that it may give grace to those who hear."* Imagine what your marriage would be like if you would just do that? When Jesus speaks through me, He wants to speak words of grace and kindness and redemption and healing and blessing. Those are words that edify and lift up. Like your grandparents used to say, "If you don't have anything nice to say, don't say anything at all."

You can't live with a referee. You can't have a live-in marriage counselor in your spare bedroom for whenever you need to talk something through. You have to learn how to speak to each other in a way that will create a safe atmosphere—where you can both be candid without pushing each other's buttons and setting off another argument.

And it's not only about what you say, but also about how you say it. As we have counseled couples, we've discovered that about 85 percent of communication challenges are caused by the wrong tone of voice, and that most of the time the person talking doesn't even realize the contempt or frustration they are expressing through how they are speaking.

There are several different layers of communication operating at once when we talk with one another. I like to say we communicate verbally, non-verbally, and para-verbally. Verbally is the words we choose, non-verbally are the gestures we add to that, and para-verbally is our tone of voice or how we can just nod our heads and go, "Uh, huh. Yeah. Uh, huh."

Think about the many bad attitudes your voice inflection and body language are capable of communicating. There's disrespect, anger, hatred, bitterness, contempt, vengeance, fear, anxiety, pride, condescension, harshness, superiority, self-righteousness, sarcasm, criticism, callousness, impatience, and indifference, just to name a few. When I call Billie from another room, she can tell immediately whether I have a simple inquiry, am upset about something, or getting ready for a tirade. She can tell all of that simply by the way I say her name. If she says she needs to talk to me, I can tell right away if we're about to have a heart to heart when I need to just listen and let her work things out as she talks, or if she is looking for my insights into a situation and wants to hear what I have to say. With just an inflection, I can communicate to her love, acceptance, and compassion, or my demeanor can communicate forgiveness, patience, humility, or gentleness. We have to keep the *way* we communicate with each other from interfering with our conversations as much as the *words* we choose to use.

We have to keep the way we communicate with each other from interfering with our conversations as much as the words we choose to use.

Learn Your Spouse's Communication Style

When Billie and I first got married, she really wasn't a communicator. She has always been a quiet person, and is quite content to take everything in and not say a word. We used to travel a good deal in our own bus to minister in different places around the country after our children were grown, and she could sit looking out the window all the way from Texas to California without saying a word. Me, I prefer a running commentary. I like to narrate the entire trip. If she gives directions from Houston to our ranch, she'll say, "Get on 59 south and drive until you get to El Campo. Take 71 to the left when you get to the Shell station and come out seventeen miles." I would give a string of landmarks from the Houston Airport all the way to our doorstep and it would take about 20 minutes if the person is willing to listen that long. We just communicate differently.

Because of this, it is easy for me to overwhelm her when we speak if I don't actively work to listen with my heart and not just my ears. Because I'm a talker, it's easy for me to forget that our conversation is a dialogue and not a monologue. I think a lot of men have this same tendency. It's not just about listening, it's about hearing too. You listen with your ears, but hear with your heart. That is a different level of engagement.

Another challenge I experienced earlier in our marriage is that I would try to interpret for Billie rather than letting her say what she had to say and really trying to understand her point of view before I responded. I would assume I knew what she was thinking before she spoke—or subconsciously devalue her ideas as she presented them. I have found that many men in Christian circles cling tightly to Ephesians 5:23 (ESV), *"For the husband is the head of the wife even as Christ is the head of the church…"* thinking that being the head means he is the sole person who has to make all of the decisions. But any head that does not consider the rest of the body—especially the heart—is undermining its own success. That's not leadership, it's insecurity.

But any head that does not consider the rest of the body—especially the heart— is undermining its own success.

Every wife has valuable input to give to every decision that affects the family. However, I used to have preconceived ideas of how I wanted things to go or I had already made up my mind about what I wanted to do, so when I came to discuss it with Billie, I turned the conversation into a monologue. I would listen with my ears, but while she was talking I was already formulating my next question or argument against what she was saying. Or I would interpret for her. I would interrupt her in midsentence and say something like, "No, no, no; that is not what you mean to say. This is what you are really trying to say."

But the truth is every time I interrupted her, I was really missing what she was saying, missing a perspective outside of my own, full of insights I didn't have. I was missing a whole different set of perceptions and intuitions I could have benefitted from to make better choices. I was shutting down what her heart was trying to tell mine.

I think that most husbands and wives need to realize that there's nobody on the planet who wants the best for them like their spouse does, and oftentimes that spouse can see things more clearly because he or she is not blinded by the other's "me-my-I-self" defenses and insecurities. Too often we are so full of ourselves we don't want to acknowledge that our spouse knows things we don't, or that they can hear things from God that we don't hear. I believe you can be blinded to the things you're doing and you can be deaf to what you're saying. That's why we need to learn to trust each other's input. If your spouse is to complete you, then they will add value to your life, make up where you lack, fill in the gaps, and see what you can't see. We have to realize that—apart from the Holy Spirit—the best advisor we have on this earth is our spouse, and to receive that counsel, we have to really hear with our hearts.

To hear in this way means to let our walls of defense down. It means to open up our hearts to what the other is saying and honestly consider it before formulating a response. And it means to talk things through to resolution, not just regulate issues to keep the damage to a minimum. I don't mean talking things to death, but talking them through to some kind of consensus.

Instead, so many people are avoiders. They think by avoiding and not addressing certain issues they are going to go away. They never do though, they just get worse. Couples who are in the avoidance habit build up emotional inertia over time that is like uranium of the soul—heavy and explosive. Rather, we should be making molehills out of mountains. I believe that any time we come to an impasse in our relationship, we need to stop right there to talk things through and clear disagreements away.

Billie and I don't always end up on the same page when we talk about things, but when we give each other the opportunity to share the other's heart in an atmosphere of mutual respect and love, we each become more cognizant of what we need to do to help the other work through whatever the struggle is. Too many marriage counselors make communication into a list of do's and don'ts to "check off" instead of teaching couples to value what the other is saying at the level of the heart.

We also have to remember that even if we are on the same page, we are still different people in different places mentally, emotionally, and spiritually. What God is opening up to you is seldom what He is working on with your spouse. I remember when I first got saved, I would get so excited about some message I was listening to on tape, but when I played it for Billie, it wouldn't affect her the same way. It was no big deal. Or she would give me a book to read that really made an impression on her, but I would get bored with it halfway into the first chapter. I know of women who keep books laying around the house or on the bed stands hoping their husbands will pick them up to read. But listen, even if the husband does read it, he's not going to get the same thing out of it because it's not likely on the subject God is working him through at that moment.

We cannot be the Holy Spirit to each other. We can pray for each other, but we can only work on changing ourselves, not each other. So make sure *you* are growing and leave your spouses growth to God. Only then will you have the peace and trust necessary to have the difficult conversations required to transform your marriage.

CHAPTER 11

TWO SHIPS PASSING IN THE KITCHEN

The goal in marriage is not to think alike, but to think together. —Robert C. Dodds

*E*very couple needs to have a regular time where they clear everything else away and sit down to talk without distractions. Times they can focus on listening to each other without other concerns on their minds. One of the most corrosive habits we have seen couples fall prey to is talking about important issues while they are passing like ships in the night. They are getting ready to go to work in the morning and the wife will say, "Oh, by the way, momma's sick again and I was thinking she could move into the spare room—you know, we could put her bed in there and all the medical equipment—but we can talk about that tonight." We drop bombs when there is no time to defuse them—and by doing so, all we do is drive shrapnel into each other because there is no chance for resolution. We talk about important things that are too important to holler across the room while the other is hurrying off to work or to drive the kids to school.

We've also noticed that a lot of couples will try to use their kids to reach their spouse. They will tell their kids, "If your father would just do this," or "If your mother wouldn't always overreact so much when I try to talk to her about that." Your children are not your sounding board for what's in your heart—nor are your parents or your in-laws—your spouse is. You can't talk to a third party hoping your spouse will get the message because you don't think they will accept it from you.

Oftentimes such things arise because you have chosen an inopportune time to try to communicate. Your spouse, despite their best intentions, seems to slough it off because they were in the middle of something else—or they didn't have time in that instant to drop everything and give you their full attention. You have to place value on communicating by being willing to pick a time when you are both in the right frame of mind to sit down, pray together, and then open your hearts to each other about what is going on in your lives. This is the only way you can truly bring each other up to speed about what you're doing and where you are emotionally.

So Much to Talk About, So Little Time

Practically speaking, what are some things that couples can do? Life is so busy. Often, especially if you have kids with activities, work obligations, and commitments outside of the family like church or community groups, there doesn't seem to be enough hours in the day to sit down and have an in-depth conversation. However, you've got to put things on hold regularly while you sit down and reason concerns out together.

Set aside one night during the week when you can lower your defenses and talk about issues without interruption. Recognize you want the best for each other despite all of your conflicting personal desires and outside commitments. That is not something you can do in passing—you have to mentally prepare yourself not to react and not to let your buttons be pushed, and that takes a special atmosphere that doesn't exist when you are trying to do something else or the kids are vying for your attention. You've got to filter through your own emotions and your own paradigm whether or not this is the right time. Unfortunately, due to our schedules, this is something many couples can only work into slowly over time.

I like to use this analogy to explain the attitude necessary for this process: if you take a spoon and face it toward you, you will be looking at the concave side of the spoon. When you do this, you're going to see yourself upside down and backward. You raise your right hand to wave, but you see it backward. Not only that, but everything points directly back at you. This is a self-centered, self-consumed, self-absorbed perspective, and when you relate to others like that, everything is always upside down, backward, and catawampus.

But if I turn the spoon around, I see it convexly. Suddenly I can see everything more correctly. I wave my hand on the right and it's on the right, not upside down or backward. However, when I do this the spoon is now focused on the other person, not on myself. My attitude is focused on what is best for the other, on blessing the other, on adding value to their life. So there's only two ways to look at things: concavely or convexly. Either everything is pointed back toward you upside down, or pointed toward the other person right side up.

Jesus always related to others convexly, not concavely. He was always serving others, adding value to their lives, helping and blessing others. For this to happen, there needs to be a willingness in each spouse's heart to work through to where they can sit down and talk, putting aside personal agendas, dropping defenses, forgetting past hurts, and working through issues so that their marriage can become better for the sake of each other, their children, their futures, and the glory of God.

We really think couples should try to either write things down or put off discussing them until they can sit down and talk together at a time when they are not in a rush or engaged in some other activity. When they are both in a mind-set to communicate with open hearts is the time to talk. Sometimes just putting off an important discussion, or writing down an issue that seems pressing at the moment, can alleviate some of the intensity of it—the immediate tension will dissipate enough so that emotion won't cloud reason.

It's not always necessary to resolve every issue right away—especially regarding decisions you have some time to think about—but you do need to know where each other stands and you can only do that by openly communicating regularly. Sometimes there is no immediate resolution. Sometimes you will have to repeatedly mull an issue over together until you can agree on the right course of action—but even conversations that need to be repeated should be done so in love and with patience.

Can You Hear Me Now?

I can tell when Billie's ready to listen, and she can tell when I'm ready to listen. By the time you've been married a few years, you should know when your spouse is ready to hear what you have to say or sense when there is something they need to talk about. Then when your spouse says he or she needs to talk to you about something, if you can at that moment, you need to be able to sit down and be ready to hear; if you can't, then you need to be sure to do it before you head to bed that night. There are no excuses for not taking care of your most important relationship before anything else.

For a wife to fulfill her role as a sanctuary to her husband's heart, she must be willing to listen to him through all of his hurts and heartaches. She can help keep a conversation from being a negative time of complaining and whining—there is always a way to talk positively about negative situations. Resist the temptation to shift blame or talk about how hopeless things are. Infuse your conversations with faith. Have the courage to talk about the things you'd rather avoid. Avoiding issues is not going to resolve them, but if you can learn to talk positively about them, you'll be on your way to a robust and resilient marriage.

There is always a way to talk positively about negative situations.

Don't get to the end of your marriage and regret not having communicated more with your husband or wife, or don't allow that lack of communication to end your marriage!

Until I really turned my life over to God after my failure in the mid-1980s, I wasn't very positive. I think three words could sum up 80 percent of my interactions with our children: "No," "Don't," and "Stop." If I had it to do all over again, the one thing

I would change is hearing and communicating in a more positive and productive way. I would have opened my heart to hear more of their hopes, their dreams, and their fears. I would have taken more time to share my own hopes, dreams, and fears. Before I could do that, however, I had to be secure enough in my relationship with God that, if they disagreed with me, I wouldn't go ballistic on them. That took some real change in *me* before that was possible.

What if They Knew the Real Me?

Oftentimes we are paralyzed by unspoken questions. "What will my mate think of me if he or she knew this or that about the way I felt?" The fear of being rejected or condemned keeps us from sharing deeply. We are afraid we will lose the respect of our partners, although this should never be so. Fear of rejection is a big part of why couples don't talk. However, since we should value our spouse's respect more than anyone else's, we must find a way to be open to receiving their "confessions" with an attitude of forbearance and forgiveness. This is our opportunity to extend God's love to our husbands or our wives when they are at their most vulnerable, and many breakthroughs in marriage happen when this level of communications is available.

What we want to do is help set our spouses and our children free to become who God wants them to be. You don't have to force your family members to be like you and think like you in order for you to love each other. Let me say that again: You have to like each other, but you don't have to be like each other, to love each other.

You have to like each other, but you don't have to be like each other, to love each other.

That doesn't mean you are independent of each other either. We believe in being *interdependent* upon each other. I am dependent upon Billie for certain things and she depends upon me for certain things. We are interdependent upon each other and also dependent upon the Lord. But for this to work, you can't go months at a time without opportunities for face-to-face, heart-to-heart communication.

Post a "No Fishing" Sign

After we have counseled with a couple, we try to get them to draw a line between what has happened before and what will happen from then on. We tell them to "Leave the past in the lake and post a 'no fishing' sign." When they are with us, they have to get everything out from the past and deal with it while under our counsel; but after that, there is no going back to cover that ground over and over and over again. If you do, you are not going to make progress because there is no way to undo what has already been done. As the apostle Paul says in Philippians 3:13-14 (ESV), *"One thing I do: forgetting what lies behind and straining forward to what lies ahead, press on toward the goal for the prize of the upward call of God in Christ Jesus."* Once you have asked forgiveness and forgiven each other, leave it all in the lake and put away your fishing rod. Don't even look to see if the fish are biting. If you do, you'll deny yourself the opportunity to change.

As one couple we counseled put it, "Instead of getting hysterical, we get historical." Anytime they would have an argument, it wasn't long before one of them went back and brought up some offense from ancient history. "Do you remember that time we were going down the road and you looked at that woman on December 5th, 1976?" "I don't remember that." "Well, I do!" How do you ever move on in your relationship when you are stuck in 1976? As that old country western song says, "There ain't no future in the past."

Religion teaches self-denial, but Christianity is about denial of self.

We're not suggesting denying issues. Nor are we advocating self-denial, but we do believe in *denial of self.* Religion teaches self-denial, but Christianity is about denial of self—denial of the desires of the "me-my-I-self" to put you before your spouse. The reason for the contrast is that religion sees *things* as the issue, but Christianity teaches *self* is the issue. A lot of people think they are doing things right if they deny themselves cigarettes, booze, or some other vice that is harmful, but they still allow themselves to be spiteful, bitter, selfish, and contentious. They give in to self and they are no better for it because, while avoiding bad exterior things is good, they are not the corrupting issue—selfishness is the corrupting issue.

If I can walk in victory in Jesus over self, if I can "die to self," then those outer things that corrupt the body aren't going to be the issue, but neither are the inner things that corrupt the heart.

If there are any touchy subjects in your relationship that you can't breach the gap to talk about, you need to get help to open up the communication lines. There must not be any issue that you can't touch—nothing so fragile that you can't bridge that gap to discuss it openly with each other. With the help of a counselor, you can open the Pandora boxes in your marriage and battle whatever comes out. But once those things are out and you have talked them through to resolution, put them back in their boxes, nail the lids shut, and leave them with the counselor.

Top Ten Communication Strategies for a Lasting Marriage

If we are going to learn to enjoy our marriage relationship rather than simply endure it, once we have torn down the "me-my-I-self" wall, we'll need to remember the basic principles of communication. Here they are once more in an easy-to-digest list:

1. Deal with unresolved past issues honestly, transparently, redemptively, and lovingly, with forgiveness.

2. Hear with your heart rather than only listening with your ears.

3. Realize that not everything is an issue. People are in

different places spiritually and mentally most of the time. What is impactful to you now probably won't have the same affect on them, and vice versa.

4. Understand that the greatest challenges are from within, not from without.

5. Adopt an attitude of gratitude for all the positive things in your marriage.

6. Settle in your mind that a good marriage is always one under construction.

7. Resign as general manager of the universe and let God work on you.

8. Verbally confirm your love for each other every day.

9. Believe in the power of the agape love that never fails.

10. Pray that your marriage relationship will bring glory to God.

It's Worth Talking Things Through

A husband and wife cannot walk away from each other just because it's no longer "fun" to be together. That's not the way God designed marriage, and it's not the commitment you made to each other when you got married. We cannot build walls to keep our mates away when it hurts to be open with one another. We must be willing to pull down those walls and be vulnerable. God has given us the means to go through anything with one another—His *agape* love. When we show each other this forgiving love, we will see our relationship grow stronger as a result. There can be no such thing as a fragile relationship in a marriage. Only deep enduring relationships that are centered on and cemented together by covenant commitment and communication produce a love that lasts a lifetime.

No relationship is more susceptible to pain and hurt than the marriage relationship. We know each other better than anybody else knows us; and because of that, it is easier for us to hurt and manipulate each other more than anyone else. I know just what I can say to Billie to hurt her. She knows just what she can say to me to hurt me. But we must, at all costs, resist pushing each other's buttons—even "accidently," convincing ourselves we didn't mean to.

If you fill your relationship with little hurtful jibes or accusations—little foxes with sharp teeth—you take the chance of consuming one another. One sarcastic comment leads to another. Each cutting remark, even if it is offered in humor, begs for reply. Soon the conflict will escalate. An innocent comment will hit a raw nerve and unleash the furor of the other person. This continual backbiting that characterizes so many relationships will eventually destroy the relationship and all that you share together if left unchecked.

A study by psychologists Cliff Nortarius and Howard Markman discovered that couples who stayed together uttered five or fewer put-downs out of every hundred comments to each other, but couples who inflicted ten or more putdowns out of every hundred comments eventually split up.[1] Sometimes we may say we're kidding, but there is almost always some underlying truth to any joke we make at someone else's expense, especially between a husband or wife. This just goes to show you that it doesn't really take much—even one statement in ten—to drive a wedge between you and your spouse. These little comments cut all the same, and we need to curb them as much as any other negative remark or criticism.

A soft answer turns away wrath,
but a harsh word stirs up anger
(Proverbs 15:1).

Proverbs 15:1 teaches, *"A soft answer turns away wrath, but a harsh word stirs up anger."* Restoration can only take place in an atmosphere of mutual confession. Every time Billie and I talk to resolution, we both end up apologizing to each other even though it's never all my fault or all her fault. There are areas in her life, areas in my life, and areas in both of our attitudes that are wrong, so we end up asking for each other's forgiveness.

We must learn to trust the honesty of our mates rather than allowing the slightest negative comment to devastate us. We should welcome their criticism and insights. If there's open dialogue and communication going on, these observations won't be inflammatory. We will know they are coming from the person who knows us best and loves us the most with a desire to see us grow.

Marriages work not because we do not hurt each other, but because when we hurt we respond with love instead of trying to hurt in return. A good marriage is not one that lacks problems, because very few ever will, but instead is built from the willingness to confront and the ability to deal with those problems as a unified force.

Communication is imperative, but it is not just listening to each other, it's hearing each other.

In God's lifelong process of molding us into who He wants us to be, our life partners are often the primary tools that He uses. The only way we can give ourselves to one another and receive from each other is through mutual submission. This attitude of placing ourselves under another person in order to give to him or her is the key to growth in all relationships, especially in our marriage relationship. Communication is imperative, but it is not just listening to each other, it's *hearing* each other. We talk through to resolution, even if things get a little "exciting" along the way. When we can do that, marriage is something that will go from one level of love to another, growing and blessing everyone who is touched by our being together.

Endnote

1. *Focus on the Family Bulletin,* May 1994.

CHAPTER 12

HUSBANDS, LOVE YOUR WIVES

Marriage is our last, best chance to grow up.
—Joseph Barth

Of the issues that challenge marriage today, one of the most confusing is the changing roles of men and women. With more women working and our traditional male-dominated society getting a significant attitude adjustment, has this also changed the way marriages should look? Should women have a more equal part in decision-making? What if the woman is more of a natural leader and the husband more of a follower— or the wife is more excitable and the man is more low-key? What if the woman works and the man stays home with the kids? Do these things justify men not being the heads of their households, or changing the traditional marriage roles in other significant ways?

The truth of the matter is that while different cultures and historical periods may have a slightly different interpretation of Scriptures, it is still Scripture that should dictate our attitudes and the way we carry ourselves, not cultural norms. At the same time, the role changes of recent decades may actually return many families to a more Christ-like pattern than the traditional Christian views of the past.

As I have said already, men are to be the head of their families, but being a head that lords control over the rest of the family is not the pattern God had in mind when He first instituted marriage. His example has always been that the husband should love and serve the wife just as Jesus has the Church. While there is no question that Jesus is the Head of the Church, He defined that relationship very differently when He chose to call His disciples friends rather than servants in John 15:15-16 (ESV):

No longer do I call you servants, for the servant does not know what his master is doing; but I have called you friends, for all that I have heard from my Father I have made known to you. You did not choose me, but I chose you and appointed you that you should go and bear fruit and that your fruit should abide, so that whatever you ask the Father in my name, he may give it to you. (John 15:15-16 ESV))

Again, as we discussed in Chapter 2, this is what is meant by covenant friendship—an *agape* relationship of always wanting to bless the other. He was telling His disciples that He was not going to hide things from them, but be open and honest in His leadership—that ministry together would be a partnership, not a dictatorship. In regard to those who want to be in charge, Jesus says, *"If anyone desires to be first, he shall be last of all and servant of all"* (Mark 9:35). This is the pattern for being responsible for the family as well.

One Spirit, One Body, One Flesh, but Two Minds

When God created the first marriage, He took a rib out of man's side and made for him a companion Adam describes as *"bone of my bones and flesh of my flesh"* (Gen. 2:23). What was one became two, and opportunity for the first marriage relationship was created—the first human covenant was formed between the first man and the first woman. That marriage would be the reuniting of the two into one, *"Therefore a man shall leave his father and mother and be joined to his wife, and they shall become one flesh"* (Gen. 2:24). This "flesh of my flesh" or "one flesh" principle is at the core of the concept of marriage.

The Kingdom of God is a Kingdom of right relationships. Every challenge we have in our life is because we refuse or confuse our threefold relationship—our relationship with God, others, and things. We are:

- Under God by faith.

- Equal to each other in love.

- Over things as stewards.

We are not equal to God or over God—we are *under* Him. We are not inferior or superior to others—we are *equal*. Things are not more important or as important than people—people are *over* things. To confuse these three relationships is to not understand the Kingdom of God.

God's glory is revealed in the context of relationship. God's qualities of love, mercy, goodness—all the fruit of the Spirit for that matter—would be useless if there were no one with whom to relate (see Gal. 5:22-23). When God created Adam, the only thing He saw missing was someone with whom Adam could be in relationship. God said, *"It is not good that man should be alone; I will make him a helper comparable to him"* (Gen. 2:18). Helper in this sense has the meaning of "other self"—a reflection or mirror image with whom Adam could see face to face. This face-to-face concept is especially important in the context of marriage because it also represents exclusivity. You can only be face to face with one person at a time. We get the same sense of meaning from the term eye to eye. When two people agree, it is said they see eye to eye. Exclusive devotion is expressed in the eyes. When we are joined together as husband and wife we are to be eye to eye and face to face.

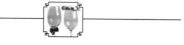

When we are joined together as husband and wife we are to be eye to eye and face to face.

A husband and wife are to be of one heart and mind just as Jesus is with His Body, the Church. The words used in Genesis 2:24, *"be united,"* in the original Hebrew carry the connotation of being glued or cemented together. As husband and wife, we are still ourselves, but we are indivisible—that is, without division. When God sees one, He sees the other—*"the two of them become like one person"* (Gen. 2:24 CEV). You do not become one person with no distinction between you, but you are so close that there is no *division* between you. God doesn't want anything to come between you and your spouse—not your children, career, ministry, community involvement, or hobbies. Marriage takes precedence over all other relationships, save Christ Himself.

When I think of marriage, I think of the apostle Paul's illustration of *"being knit together in love"* (Col. 2:2). I think of a blanket woven with two distinct colors of yarn. Although you can see the unique threads, they are always seen together and function as one. They are interlaced so that whatever happens to one happens to both—they are part of the same fabric. Spiritually, God sees you together, and is the witness between a husband and wife regarding their faithfulness to love. God relates to you in full view of that relationship.

The apostle Paul went on to use the relationship between Christ and the Church to show what marriage should look like. It is a powerful illustration of selfless giving and self-loving. I say "self-loving" because Paul likens loving your spouse to loving your self:

> ...*He who loves his wife loves himself. For no one ever hated his own flesh, but nourishes and cherishes it, just as the Lord does the church* (Ephesians 5:28-29).

The greatest picture we have of the marriage covenant is of Christ and the Church—each losing their life in the other, both gaining a richer, more abundant life in return. Jesus taught that only by losing your life will you find true life. Isn't that the basic tenet of the Gospel? That when you surrender your life to Christ, He gives you His resurrected life in exchange? That is the mystery and beauty of your marriage relationship as well—when you surrender your lives to one another, your life is returned with a greater capacity to love.

In light of this we are told, *"The husband is the head of the wife even as Christ is the head of the church, His body, and is Himself its Savior. Now as the church submits to Christ, so also wives should submit in everything to their husbands"* (Eph. 5:23-24 ESV). We see that the husband's headship is about servant-leadership, not to make servants of his household. He is to be the rock upon which his wife can depend, trusting he always wants the best for her. As a husband gives himself to his wife and serves her and encourages her and affirms her, she grows in beauty and grace. He presents her to himself the way he desires her to be as a result of his mercy and love.

Every man must look at his wife after 30 years and know that he has contributed to that woman. She is becoming what he has helped her to become—and hopefully that will be something wonderful! If she is growing in beauty, it is because of his faithfulness and love. If she fails to measure up to his hopes, it is because he has failed to give her the love she needs to flourish.

Thus, as the "head," he is the leader who wants to see his wife growing in beauty, virtue, and success. The man is responsible to set things in order in his home so that everyone in it will prosper. He is responsible to initiate the tough conversations with his wife when things aren't going so well. He's responsible to make sure issues are dialogued through to resolution. It is his responsibility to hear his wife with his heart, not just his ears.

As the head of the home, he is responsible to God for the spiritual well-being of his wife and children, and when something is not right, it is his job to intercede in prayer just as Jesus does for the church.

Now, if his wife decides she's going to be contentious and stubborn, and dig her heels in to be the leader of the family, then it's going to take a lot of prayer, a lot of discipline, a lot of self-sacrifice, and a lot of forgiveness, but the man's responsibilities don't change. You don't throw your children away because they are rebellious—you must love and discipline them until they understand the evil nature of rebellion and accept your authority once again.

Neither do you discard your wife because she doesn't hunker down under your authority—and you don't treat her like a child. She is your wife, *not* your child. Most of the time if the woman is not following her husband's lead, it is because he is not leading the family anywhere worth going! So the mandate for the husband is not to quote her a bunch of Scriptures about how she needs to submit to him, but to go and get with God like Moses on the mountaintop and start leading in a direction she can't help but get behind!

*We're responsible as men to make
our marriage relationships work,
and no finger pointing at our wives
is going to change that.*

We're responsible as men to make our marriage relationships work, and no finger pointing at our wives is going to change that. After all, you can't control her, you can only control you. If you are going to change something, then it will have to be your example and the way you love and lead. If you look and see things about her you don't like, you get before God and ask Him to show you *your* heart and the things that need to change in *your* life. Be honest with God about the way you treat her. Be honest about the way you minister to her and your children. If you do that, eventually you will see His light invading your relationships and making things better. You will come home and see the rats and cockroaches (the little issues eating away at your marriage) scurrying out of your home to escape the light.

This is not to say that wives aren't responsible to honor and respect their husbands, and to submit to them as unto the Lord—but at the same time, it is not the husband's job to *make* his wife submit. *Submission* is a word that's fallen on hard times today, but it is still an important biblical concept. We're to be in submission to those that are in authority over us.

In the Gospel according to Matthew, Jesus recognized that a Roman officer's understanding of authority and his ability to submit to it was the basis of his "great faith." As the story is told in Matthew 8:5-13, when the centurion came to Jesus that day, he asked, *"I've got a servant at home sick. Would you heal him?"* Jesus said, *"I'll go with you."* He said, *"No, no, I too am a man under authority and I say to this man go and he goes and this man come and he comes. Speak the word only and he will be healed."* At that, Jesus turned to His disciples and said, *"I've not seen so great faith, no not in all of Israel."* Jesus equated great faith with somebody who understood the power of submitting to authority.

This same kind of faith is needed in our homes as well. When a woman submits to her husband as unto the Lord, she is exercising that kind of faith. If a husband is wrong in the course he has set for the family, God will correct him—if he is wrong in how he is living day to day, God will chasten him. But if she is in rebellion against her husband, she is not trusting God in *His* leadership. This takes her outside of the umbrella of protection He provides through her husband and the authority He has given him to lead in the home. Once again, the husband being the head doesn't mean that a woman is inferior. She is intrinsically equal in every way. However, since God is not a God of chaos but a God of order, He has appointed the man as the leader because you cannot have two heads without creating a monster!

The most important thing a husband can do for his family is to love the mother of his children.

That said, the most important thing a husband can do for his family is to love the mother of his children. He will not only cultivate her strengths, but also allow her to compensate for his weaknesses. If a father wants to show his children how they should act in a loving and obedient way in the home, he needs to love and lead his wife—sacrificing his own selfish desires and praying for her regularly—just as Jesus does for His Church.

That kind of servant-leadership gives stability to a family—a stability that allows children to thrive and give the wife the confidence she needs to trust him to do his best on their behalf. When a wife can trust her husband to lead like God intended him to, she can easily yield to his authority and work together with him for the good of all. Submission shouldn't be a strenuous, difficult thing—it should be natural and easy, like following the lead when partnering in a dance.

When Jesus spoke about us being submitted to His leadership, He said, *"Take My yoke upon you and learn from Me, for I am gentle and lowly in heart, and you will find rest for your souls. For My yoke is easy and My burden is light"* (Matt. 11:29-30 NIV). When Jesus said, "My yoke is *easy* and My burden is *light,*" He was making it simple. If my yoke is *difficult* and my burden *heavy*, then I am not properly related to Him. I don't know about you, but we like easy and light, not difficult and heavy.

This is how it should be between husbands and their wives. A husband should be able to say to his wife, *"...Walk with me and work with me—watch how I do it. Learn the unforced rhythms of grace. I won't lay anything heavy or ill-fitting on you. Keep company with me and you'll learn to live freely and lightly"* (Matt. 11:29-30 MSG). This is how he should be leading in the great dance of marriage.

CHAPTER 13

THE BASIC NEEDS OF A WOMAN

An ideal wife is any woman who has an ideal husband.
—Booth Tarkington

*E*ven if the marriage was made in Heaven, the husband is still responsible for the maintenance. It is still up to him to lead and care for his wife—and her well-being and satisfaction in life is a reflection of how well he is doing his job.

When I officiate over a wedding ceremony, I always share Isaiah 62:5, *"As the bridegroom rejoices over the bride, so shall your God rejoice over you."* Does that mean if you are not rejoicing over your wife that God isn't rejoicing over you? No, of course not. But it does mean you should be delighting in your wife in the same way God delights in you. In other words, God is paying attention and is mindful of all you are doing, and it brings Him great pleasure. All you do doesn't go unnoticed. He doesn't take you for granted.

The husband is the "house band." It is his job to bind the home together.

The *husband* is the "house band." It is his job to bind the home together. As Christ holds the Church together as one universal Body on the earth, so the husband binds the members of the home together as a family. He's the prophet in the home to give direction. He's the priest. He's the spiritual intercessor. He's the provider—the one who makes sure the home has enough of everything that it needs. Even though today we live in a world where women work and some even make more money than their husbands, he is still primarily responsible to see that needs are met—just as she is primarily responsible to nurture and care for the children. That doesn't mean husbands and wives don't both play a role in all aspects of running a household. A smart husband will recognize the gift he has in his wife, the discernment and insight she has to offer, the prayer support she can provide, and will make decisions with her input and wisdom.

The husband is not only the main provider, but also the protector. He's the one who must discern where enemies are lurking or where defenses are weak. He must not only keep watch against intruders, but also "run the fences" to make sure there are no breaches or weak areas. A husband needs to discern where a woman may be vulnerable and protect her in that area. He will see things she does not, just as she will see things he does not. We all have blind spots. It is up to the husband to make sure open, honest dialogue about such issues is possible, and that he and his wife trust the other enough to learn from and grow with each other.

The husband should be the reliable friend in the home. I believe the husband is to be the prophet, priest, provider, protector, and the *pal* in the home. From my perspective, I think that most of the challenges in the home stem from the fact that the husband is not the kind of head that God has anointed and ordained and challenged him to be. And if he would be, I believe that most of the challenges in our marriage relationships would be resolved.

Do you know what most wives are looking for in a husband? They are seeking a faithful, loving, compassionate, understanding, listening individual who will confidently lead the home—not a wimp! I don't think most women want somebody they can control.

Husbands are the sons of Adam and wives are daughters of Eve. Just as Eve wanted the best for Adam, wives want the best for their husbands. They may go about achieving what they think is best in a willful way, but they are only trying to be proactive in bringing to pass their vision for a great marriage. They don't want to take control of the husband as much as they want the husband to take control of the marriage and make it something great. I think most wives simply get frustrated because their husbands aren't being proactive enough—they are simply trying to get them to step up to the plate. The last thing most women want is to be married to a wimp.

In a good number of the couples we counsel, the women are hard chargers and their husbands are not. If the husband doesn't stand up to take the leadership role, these women will move into it by default and things in the family will get out of balance quickly. When this happens, the husband feels henpecked, but the truth is that the woman is trying to get her man to take his place—she is doing it in the wrong way, but that is the motivation in her heart, whether she realizes that or not. She's trying to push her husband into leadership, even if it is in a rebellious way. She instinctively wants him to be the one who watches over the home, even if she is acting contrary to that.

In many ways, it is like the way the movie *Instinct* puts it. Anthony Hopkins lived among the gorillas for years and years and had a hard time coming back and reentering human society because he had been away so long. When the psychologist, played by Cuba Gooding Jr., finally gets him talking, the Hopkins' character makes the following statement:

> She was a good mother and a good teacher. The baby was always protected, always instructed. Always groomed, always…touched, safe. She used to watch over him, *the way the old silverback used to watch over…all of us, even me.*

It's an amazing…feeling, Theo, to be watched over.

That's the way that I see the husband's role. He is the one who watches over the family. He watches over the relationships, the finances, the provision, the protection—everything. He does it because he is called to be the leader and it is his responsibility to see that things are going well. That's the role that God gave him: to watch over the family and be godly enough to discern the challenges in the family and then set the correct course to avoid or overcome them.

I believe there are basically seven needs a woman has that her husband is to watch over and take responsibility for:

1. Spiritual leadership.

2. Personal affirmation.

3. Affection.

4. Intimate conversation.

5. Mutual honesty and transparency.

6. Stability and support.

7. To know her husband is committed to their family.

These are the needs the husband agrees to fulfill when he asks her to marry him. While he has needs as well, it is not up to him to determine how his wife meets his needs, only how he meets hers. That is what God calls husbands to do when He commands husbands to love their wives as Christ loves the Church. The husband and father is responsible to see over the needs of the wife and children and manage the quality of relationships and the general morale within the home.

We have friends right now that when they die, they're going to die knowing that their children are at odds with each other—that they disdain each other. I don't want that! I want to go knowing that despite whatever challenges my children might have with each other, they are still dedicated to each other. I believe protecting and developing those relationships is a big part of a father's responsibility.

Being a Husband is a Full-time Job

I know that being a husband is a full-time job. There is really never a time when he is off-duty—even when he is not with his family, he has responsibilities he needs to be constantly aware of. He still needs to be accountable for what he looks at and what he says about his wife and children to other people. His spiritual integrity is not something that is determined by how he acts when others are looking, but how he acts all of the time. Do I think a woman has responsibilities too? You bet! But I believe that God places a greater responsibility on the man, because to whom much is given, much is required.

If you invest yourself in your marriage and family, that is where your heart will be and your family will become your delight. The key to wisely ministering to your marriage is to: First, remain occupied with them when you are with them, not preoccupied with work or hobbies or television or something else. Clarify your goals and responsibilities for yourself as a husband and stick to them with conviction. It is easy to become absorbed with your job and outside activities because of their potential for achievement, accomplishment, approval, and recognition. Frankly, managing relationships at work, especially if you are the one signing the paychecks, is easier than managing those at home. It is also easier to get positive feedback regularly at work than it is at home. There is often great satisfaction in solving all of the world's problems at work, but even though you may feel that you are the only one in the universe who can do it, God doesn't hold you personally responsible for that—He *does* hold you personally responsible for your marriage and family.

Realize that "quality time" is "quantity time." No excuses.

Second, realize that "quality time" is "quantity time." No excuses. Your marriage and family are first, not next after whatever it is you want or "need" to do. Make a priority of spending time with your family every day.

Third, you must be the one to initiate open conversations with your wife instead of peacefully coexisting with her. Concentrate on building face-to-face intimacy as discussed in a previous chapter, not just side-by-side companionship. Be courageous in this area. Stay with it. Don't be a wimp!

Fourth, and finally, a "one-woman man" that ministers to his marriage has a program of prevention instead of procrastination. He recognizes and responds to danger signals that signify he may be neglecting his walk with God or his walk with his wife *before* any damage is done. Did you get that? There are two distinct things that he does: he *recognizes* and he *responds*. As the husband, you must set the parameters on the alarms that warn you danger is present.

Dealing With Temptation

When temptation comes, a man is generally seduced through his eyes and a woman is seduced through her ears. It's what a woman hears that draws her into the wrong kinds of relationships, while with a man it is what he sees. Because of this, women may fall into the wrong kind of relationship with another man and it won't even be a physical one. It will be one of inordinate affection—an unnatural attachment to another person who is not her husband. This will have happened because she has listened to him say things that meet her emotional needs, and eventually what another man says become things that only her husband should be saying to her. She will feel, "Well, he listens to me—he really understands me—and my husband doesn't!" A wife has a need to be heard with an understanding ear, and when she is not getting that at home, she will be tempted to find it elsewhere.

Men, on the other hand, must watch what they set their eyes upon. There are a lot of things in this world that you are better off not looking at because of where they take your thought life. Some may say it is not a big deal, but only you can be the judge. This can be different for different men, but if you find yourself trying to justify looking at something, you have probably already stepped over a line somewhere that you shouldn't have. Here are some of the most obvious danger signals that something is not as it should be in your life:

- When you are too busy for your wife.

- When you are too busy to spend at least one relaxed evening with the family per week (no excuses!).

- When you feel that you deserve more attention at home than you are getting.

- When you are reading or looking at things that you wouldn't want your wife or friends to know about.

- When the romance in your marriage is fading.

- When some woman says things to you that would make your wife uncomfortable.

- When a woman makes herself available to you.

- When women are attracted to you and you are tempted to make the most of it.

- When your fantasy life becomes pornographic.

- When Scriptures about adultery are for other people, not for you.

- When you start feeling sorry for yourself in regard to how your wife is compared to other women.

- When you have rationalized your behavior to the point that you hope God is not looking or listening.

Do these seem unfair? Beware my friend! If you feel that way, you may already be in danger. If you don't bring your mind and your thoughts into captivity, they will end up in the gutter—and so will your relationships.

Seven Hedges to Protect the One-Woman Man

No matter how strong we think we are, we are all subject to temptation if we allow the right circumstances to take place. The wise man, the one-woman man, recognizes the powers of his needs and desires and the danger of self-deception. He is not foolish enough to believe that he can expose himself to and successfully endure needless temptation. Maturity is not measured by your ability to resist temptation, but rather your wisdom in avoiding it. As Proverbs 22:3 (ESV) puts it, *"The prudent sees danger and hides himself, but the simple go on and suffer for it."* There is no deception like self-deception, and the man who believes that he is not vulnerable to temptation to the point that he willfully and carelessly exposes himself to it has deceived himself. His fall is imminent.

There is no deception like self-deception.

Realizing the frailty of our nature and our weakness to temptation, a one-woman man builds fences of protection around himself—lines never to be crossed—for the sake of his marriage, his children, his credibility, and his destiny.

Hedge #1

Stay away from any "flesh" that is not your wife. Avoid pornography: hard porn (books, magazine, movies) and soft porn (television, the Internet, chat rooms, etc.). Don't go to places that immoral women frequent. In fact, avoid anything that arouses desires that cannot be morally satisfied.

Hedge #2

Avoid being alone with a female not related to you. Stay away from any situation where you are in a room alone, even if there is someone just on the other side of the door. You never know what is on the mind of another person, or what you might be accused of. Avoid dining alone with a woman you are not related to. There is something about the fellowship of a meal shared together that warrants extreme caution. Two is company and in such cases, three is security and safety. Avoid traveling one-on-one with another woman. The appearance of evil should be enough to discourage the mature man from this practice anyway. The time alone, the temptation of intimate conversation, and the sharing of personal and private information are just too dangerous.

Hedge #3

Never allow another woman to meet a need that should be met by your wife. Whether that be a shoulder massage, intimate conversation, the purchase of personal items, praying together, one-on-one counsel, inside jokes or comments to one another, or other things that only you and your wife should be engaging in, however small it may seem.

Hedge #4

In the same way, never allow yourself to meet the needs of another woman that should be met by her husband. A woman can grow vulnerable to anyone she perceives to understand her better than her husband does. It is possible to steal the affections of a woman even with the purest of intentions. The meeting of needs is a basis of love. When needs are met, a woman can be emotionally attracted to the provider, regardless of how unsuccessful or unattractive he may be.

Hedge #5

Hug only dear friends and relatives, and even that should only be done in the presence of others. When you hug someone, do it appropriately: limit touch—bend from the waist and touch a shoulder or cheek only—and limit the time—a hug that lingers too long invites inordinate thoughts.

Hedge #6

Be careful with compliments. Compliments concerning changeable features (clothes, hairstyles, character) are OK, but compliments concerning the person themselves, especially unchangeable features (eyes, figure, etc.) are flattery and suggest inappropriate attention. Care should also be taken regarding what compliments are received and how. As Proverbs 7:21

(ESV) says, *"With much seductive speech she persuades him; with her smooth talk she compels him."*

Hedge #7

Flirtation and suggestive conversation should be avoided, even in jesting. Flirting is playing with the emotions of another person to satisfy the needs of your own ego and have no edifying effect. Also, you never know the unmet needs in the life of another person and the danger that you are "flirting" with. Treat the emotions of women you meet with the same care you would want another man to treat your wife's emotions. Those things that are done suggestively or in jest are often "testing the water" for further pursuit and can become a serious temptation with lightning speed if received on the other end in a certain way.

Cherish Accountability

Furthermore, your program of prevention must include godly accountability. This means you must be open to receiving the concerns, inquiries, reservations, and warnings of your wife and friends as gifts and not insults or intrusions. In fact, the serious one-woman man will be sure to have a close man friend who has permission to ask often and without warning about anything he wishes concerning your walk with God or relationship with your wife. Such accountability is not a violation of privacy, it is an essential act of friendship, and any man who does not have someone like this in his life is missing both a great opportunity for partnership and an essential component of keeping your walk with God and your wife on the proper course.

I firmly believe that we don't have a woman problem or a child problem in the Church today, we have a man problem. Men unwilling—not unable—to lead as a result of a number of reasons, but none that excuse irresponsible behavior. It also seems we church men are unwilling—but not unable—to fight, unwilling—though not unable—to stand, and unwilling—though not unable—to persevere in doing what is right. Any coward can run and ask for a divorce, but real men stand and fight for the relationship they have committed to. If we don't stand for something, we'll fall for anything, and too many men I know have fallen for the lie that they can desert their families or abdicate their responsibilities without consequences. Our families are reeling in uncertainty because of this.

It is time to step up to the plate and make your marriage the one you have always dreamed it could be.

Men, it is time to be who God called you to be. It is time to step up to the plate and make your marriage the one you have always dreamed it could be.

CHAPTER 14

LONG-DISTANCE LOVE

The real act of marriage takes place in the heart, not in the ballroom or church or synagogue. It's a choice you make—not just on your wedding day, but over and over again—and that choice is reflected in the way you treat your husband or wife.
—Barbara De Angelis

*S*uccessful people do not live their lives accidently. Whether in your marriage or your business, choice, not chance, determines the outcome. You can choose what you read, where you go, who you associate with, to what you watch and listen, as well as how you treat each other. As a matter of fact, your entire life is made up of moment-by-moment choices whether you realize you have made them or not. Living up to your responsibilities is what life is all about.

*Responsibility is simply a person
responding to the ability God put
into them.*

I once heard a speaker say, "Responsibility is simply a person *responding* to the *ability* God put into them." When God writes opportunity on one side of the door, he also writes responsibility on the other. If we are to live lives free of regrets, then we must live lives of no excuses. Playing the blame game will not fly with God. We can choose to love our spouses, we can choose to honor them, and we can choose to be faithful. The little choices we make every day eventually make us—and our marriages.

*If we are to live lives free of regrets,
then we must live lives of no excuses.*

When we talk about making love last a lifetime, we are not talking about something you should do ten years from now, but what you choose to do today. Will you choose to love your spouse today? When it is hard to love your spouse, will you choose to love anyway or give up? When your spouse does something to hurt you, will you hurt back or love back? When there is something about your spouse you don't like, will you try to change him or her, or will you just work that much harder to change yourself? All of these are little, everyday choices, and what you do with them will make your marriage something beautiful, or it will just bury issues for later. Will you continue to regulate issues, or will you resolve them?

I received a phone call not long ago from a friend of mine about a couple we had counseled a few months back. They were a wonderful, wonderful husband and wife who we sensed we had helped to make some really important breakthroughs in their marriage. He was calling to tell us that for almost two months, things were really going well for them. Things were great, but now their marriage was falling apart again. I wish that was an isolated incident, but unfortunately it is not. We see it too often, and each and every time it is almost the exact same story. They did well for a while, they got along great and remembered why they had fallen in love in the first place, but all of a sudden it stopped. Why? Because they stopped putting into practice the principles we had taught them.

Couples come and work with us and then—even when we tell them what to beware of, they still leave with a preconceived notion of what things should be like. They think if they follow our instructions about intimacy and communication for a short period of time, things will be "fixed" with "no more problems." That's why so much of the time this only lasts for a few weeks. Then, after they have "tried it" for a while, something bugs them the same way it had bugged them before they came to counsel with us, and they think, "Man, this isn't working. What was I ever thinking? I give up." They put an artificial deadline on getting things to turn around, and when they are disappointed again, they throw in the towel.

When they do this, they are putting a time frame on God by saying something like, "If this doesn't work in a week, I'm just not going to put up with it any more!" But such attitudes are why people don't succeed in anything. Whatever your dream, whatever your passion, whatever your purpose, you've got to be willing to pay a price for five, ten, fifteen years or whatever time it takes to accomplish what you want. You can never know the timeframe for turning things around. To see the fruit of whatever God has put on your heart—to achieve whatever passion and purpose He has placed in you to do—you will have to be willing to go through the difficult times, pay the price, persevere, and see it through to the end.

It's the same way in a marriage relationship. The biggest reason I believe that people fail after they have counseled with us is not because we didn't give them the right information, but because they didn't give it time to work. We can give them strategies and tools and the best advice we can on how to move into their futures in both marriage and work, but if they don't stick with applying what we teach them, even the wisest, most insightful advice won't do them a lick of good.

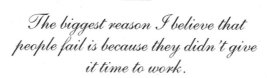

The biggest reason I believe that people fail is because they didn't give it time to work.

Or think of it this way: if I was a doctor and I gave you a prescription, and you went to the pharmacy, got the medicine, went home, and took a few of the pills, but then left the rest in the medicine cabinet, what good would that do you? It seems silly, but that has happened to me too many times not to notice the trend. We will give a couple some things to work on, some communication exercises to do together to help them open up to each other, and they'll call back a month later and say, "Listen, we need to talk. Can you counsel us some more?" Then they tell me about the very same challenges and problems we'd discussed in my office a month earlier.

I'll say, "OK, wait a minute, are you and your spouse still sitting down each week like we talked about to discuss issues and look for resolutions?"

They'll say something like, "Um, well, for a while maybe we did."

"OK then, did you do all the communication exercises we gave you?"

"Well, no, but that's not what I wanted to talk to you about. I want to talk about our problem."

Well, I think, *no wonder!*

Insanity truly is continuing to do the same things in the same way hoping for different results! If you don't change the way you are relating to your spouse, how do you ever expect a change in the challenges you are facing in your marriage?

Or, let me ask you a different question. Do you think that just because you have gone to a pastor or counselor once, you will never have emotional issues again for the rest of your life? Of course not! We are all growing and changing all the time as individuals, and no matter how hard we want some things to change, they still take time to work through. So we keep praying, we keep pushing, and we keep making the right choices, and then one day, with us hardly even stopping to realize it, things are better. It may have taken consistent effort over months or years, but things somehow did get better. And you didn't give up because you were determined to grow and change.

So, if we have made that commitment to change, why do we give up on our spouses so easily? You've got to be willing to deal with your own issues for a lifetime and be patient with you spouse as they work through theirs. For Billie and me, it took *years* to recover from the mistakes I made, but as a result our marriage is better today than it has ever been. It would have been easy to give up on it, and everyone around us probably would have been understanding and sympathetic, but it wouldn't have been the right thing to do.

If you're going to really work on your relationship for a better marriage and to honor God, there can be no time limit. You can't just *try* what we've been teaching like you try on clothing. Then when it doesn't fit anymore, you discard it. You are going to have to grow and change as an individual—and so is your marriage. You have to give it time, and you have to be determined to make the changes in yourself that will allow for the improvements to take place in your marriage.

These Principles may be Simple, but They Are Not Simplistic

Some couples struggle with these principles and practices for a better marriage, not because they are too difficult to understand, but because they are so simple they think they can't possibly work. They are things we take for granted because of their simple wisdom—like the need to sit down and communicate on a regular basis—but they think they've already tried that so it isn't going to do them any good. I read a quote some time ago that I think clearly expresses this challenge:

> Our greatest mission is to rescue admitted truths from the neglect caused by their universal admission. There is much force in this. When a truth is fighting for existence, it compels men, whether they love it or not, to consider it. But when its position is secured, it becomes like a well-used coin, or the familiar text which hangs unnoticed on the wall.[1]

We try to reinforce the same basic principles with every couple we counsel, because the truth of the matter is, this is life—Whether you're motorcycling, or mountain climbing, no matter what you're doing, there are some basic principles that apply to every aspect of life. It is only once you have mastered these basics that you can begin to put your own flair on things—that's true in business, that's true in sports, it's true in life, and it's true in marriage. They seem simplistic, they seem old hat, but they are still essential. Don't miss the profundity of what I am saying because it is simple. If you do, you will miss wisdom that will likely change your life.

*Sometimes we miss the very thing
that will make the difference because
it is not new or we have heard it a
dozen times before.*

Sometimes we miss the very thing that will make the difference for us because it is not new or we have heard it a dozen times before. Don't let that happen with these principles. They may not be new, but they will bring new life into your marriage if you will let them. There is no question, though, that *now* is the time for you to take action in faithfully applying these principles.

If Not You, then Who? If Not Now, Then When?

One of the greatest issues in the marriage relationship is when the husband neglects his responsibilities toward his wife, or the wife neglects her responsibilities toward her husband. Most marriages don't fall apart because of abuse, adultery, drunkenness, or drugs; *the number one problem that causes marital discord is neglect.* It's caused by the thing we don't pay attention to or avoid for too long. It's allowing things to stagnate rather than cultivating growth. It's by not actively pushing on into the future together, it's by not working together to continually improve your relationship.

The number one problem that causes marital discord is neglect.

If you were to leave your house for a week or two, when you came back, even though everything will be in the same place you left it, there will be dust that has settled on everything. Did someone go in and spread the dust around? Of course not! The dust is there because of neglect. You don't have to plant weeds in your garden—just by not pulling them out every week you will have so many weeds you won't be able to find your vegetables. That's what Proverbs talks about:

> *I passed by the field of a sluggard, by the vineyard of a man lacking sense, and behold, it was all overgrown with thorns; the ground was covered with nettles, and its stone wall was broken down. Then I saw and considered it; I looked and received instruction. A little sleep, a little slumber, a little folding of the hands to rest, and poverty will come upon you like a robber, and want like an armed man* (Proverbs 24:30-34 ESV).

What does neglect lead to? A miserable, broken life.

The problem is not with your spouse, it is with you.

If you neglect your relationship with your wife, neglect to work on your marriage individually and together with your wife, then bailing out on your marriage and going to find somebody else is *not* going to fix your life. Why? Because the problem is not with your spouse, it is with *you*. Whoever refuses to put in the effort to make their marriage work, or make the changes in themselves necessary for making the relationship better, is just asking for the same old problems over and over again—even if it is with a new partner.

God wants you to love your spouse the way He loves you. His forgiveness toward you is the forgiveness He wants you to extend toward your spouse. His patience, kindness, care for, and His never-ending love toward you He wants you to extend toward your family.

There is no more complicated relationship in life than that of a husband and wife—none more challenging, none more fragile. At the same time, there is none more rewarding and fulfilling. Happiness is only real when it is shared. And with whom better than the one who is your completion? I believe God intended that marriage be as much to make us holy as to make us happy.

Be happy, be holy. Choose life and love. Choose to infuse your marriage with the life and love of God. You will truly succeed at living life to the fullest simply by making your marriage all God intended it to be.

Endnote

1. James Hastings, (ed.), *The Greater Men and Women of the Bible* (New York: Charles Scribner's Sons, 1913), 479.

CHAPTER 15

A VERY PERSONAL NOTE FROM BILLIE KAYE

As for God, His way is perfect; the word of the Lord is proven [tried]; *He is a shield to all who trust in Him. For who is God, except the Lord? And who is a rock, except our God? It is God who arms me with strength, and makes my way perfect. He makes my feet like the feet of deer, and sets me on my high places* (Psalm 18:30-33).

As Paul and I were sharing our story for this marriage book, and even as I was helping proof the final draft before sending it on to the publisher, I was taken back to some of the wonderful Scriptures that encouraged me through some rough times. The Book of Psalms was especially encouraging. God's promises became so real, and I knew that I could trust that God would be my strength and help through anything and everything that Paul and I would have to walk and *work* through.

I've often said that it seems like a movie or book I read rather than my own life. God has done so much healing, and He has blessed me so greatly, that it's hard to believe I ever walked through anything other than blessing. Maybe, it's because God has done exceedingly, abundantly, above more than I could have ever asked or thought in my marriage, with our children, grandchildren, friends, and ministry. And believe me, I can ask for and think of a lot!

I've had many people ask me, "How did you do it?" I'm never really sure how to answer that question, because I'm not sure if there's one pat answer. I loved my husband! I loved my children! I wanted more than anything to please the Lord and be obedient to His Word. I wanted to make right choices for my future. I didn't want a divorce! I didn't want to leave my children without a father who was *present* with them all of the time. I didn't want to go back and live with my parents and be a burden to them. I knew I wasn't the exception—I wasn't the only woman in the world who had ever been hurt. Plus, God showed me that I needed a work in my heart as much as Paul needed a work in his. Different areas, but the same problem: *self!*

I had prayed that God would make Paul the man of God I knew he wanted and needed to be, and me the woman of God I wanted and needed to be. Well, He answered my prayer! It sure wasn't the way I wanted it answered, but He did answer! Hallelujah! He just turns us over to ourselves to show us what's inside of us—even if it's ugly—and when we see and acknowledge it, He begins to restore and heal and replace our sorrows with His beauty.

I often say to women that they need to be willing to *walk through* and *stick with* their husbands when God answers their prayers. Does it hurt? Of course! However, when we make choices based on God's Word and not on our emotions and feelings, we walk into a wonderful future with the man we prayed for— the one *God* changed—the one who is our completion!

I can say with joy in my heart that I praise God that He gave me the grace and courage to forgive. I thank Him for *everything* I have experienced, because it has brought me to where I am today. What the enemy meant for evil, God used for my good and His glory. As James Edwards says in his book *The Divine Intruder*, "God is in the business of interrupting lives and changing them forever." My heart will ever be grateful that by God's grace— which seems to be the most offensive part of the Gospel—Paul and I have a wonderful relationship and marriage today.

I have a husband who truly loves, honors, respects, provides, encourages, and prays for me. He makes me laugh—and cry, at times. I trust Him with my whole being, because I can see and hear the work that God has done in his heart. I sent Paul a card a few years back that expresses my heart. I would love to share it with you here:

Your love is everything I could ever want.
Nothing else in life could bring me as much joy as the moments we share, the memories we create, and the beautiful relationship we have built together...

No amount of material possessions could make my life as worthwhile and meaningful as you have made it.

No amount of money could buy a gift as precious.
With you in my life I have all that I could possibly want and need.

*What we share together has already made me rich beyond my
wildest dreams—opening my eyes to the true treasures in life.
No gift could compare to our hopes, our laughter, our togetherness.
Nothing else could come close to making me as happy and as loved
as I feel in your arms.*

*You mean more to me than anything that money can buy, and I want
you to know that you are all I could ever want the rest of my life.*

Deanna Laura Pool[1]

A couple of years after Paul and I had moved to North Carolina trying to rebuild our lives and ministry, we received a very hurtful letter from a "friend" who not only sent it to us, but to many pastors around the country. Many of the things in the letter were true, but much of the letter was lies and false accusations. Paul was in Russia on a mission trip at the time, so I was home with the boys and their wives.

As I read the letter, it devastated me—it zapped the life out of me. I didn't know how I could hold it together when I got back to where my kids were. But as I was driving back from the post office headed to our new condo, I looked toward the mountains surrounding Asheville. The clouds were pulling apart and the sky was beautiful. The promise of Psalm 121:1-2 came to my heart: *"I will lift up my eyes to the hills—from whence comes my help? My help comes from the Lord, Who made heaven and earth."* This so encouraged my heart that I was able to face my children without falling apart.

Later that night, I was reading *Trusting God* by Jerry Bridges. He quoted a Scripture in that book that has been a mainstay for me throughout the years: Lamentations 3:37-38 (NIV), *"Who* can speak and have it happen if the Lord has not decreed it? Is it not from the mouth of the Most High that both calamities and good things come?" I realized right then that no one could write a letter or say a word unless God *decreed* it. I knew that God was in control of everything and everyone. And that He can be trusted!

There were many who would have loved to see us out of the ministry, divorced, and destroyed, but there were some who called and spoke life and grace to us. I will ever be grateful for those who prayed for us instead of shunned us. I have absolutely no unforgiveness or anger against anyone for anything though, because I would have been one to "throw the first stone" before God did His work of grace in me. I once read, "Tougher than the transformation of the unrighteous is the transformation of the self-righteous." Boy, did that strike home! I needed a work in my heart! Whatever God chose to use to do His work of grace, I wanted to yield to His tender mercies.

> *Out of the depths I have cried to You, O Lord; Lord, hear my voice! Let Your ears be attentive to the voice of my supplications. If You, Lord, should mark iniquities, O Lord, who could stand? But there is forgiveness with You, that You may be feared. I wait for the Lord, my soul waits, and in His word I do hope* (Psalm 130:1-5).

Endnote

1. *"Your Love Is Everything I Could Ever Want"* by Deanne Laura Pool. Copyright © 1996 by Blue Mountain Arts, Inc. Reprinted by permission. All rights reserved.

CHAPTER 16

A VERY PERSONAL NOTE FROM PAUL

Have mercy upon me, O God, according to thy
lovingkindness: according unto the multitude of thy
tender mercies blot out my transgressions
(Psalm 51:1 KJV).

I end this book by sharing a few personal words that I pray
will encourage you in your journey.

Anything you do in life that is worthwhile is going to require
sacrifice. However, in all that we have been through as a couple,
I know Billie Kaye would agree that it has been worth every step
along the way for what we learned from it, both the pleasant and
unpleasant alike. As we look around at our children, our grandchildren, and our ministry—plus all of the other relationships we
have—our hearts are filled with gratitude for God's mercy in giving me a heart *willing* to change.

We are grateful for children who found God's grace to forgive a father gone astray, grateful for friends who were hurt but acted redemptively, and grateful for the people of grace who loved and encouraged us to walk in faith knowing that weeping would endure for the night, but that joy would come in the morning.

However, most of all, I am grateful for a godly wife who was violated and devastated, but found courage to trust the Lord through uncharted waters.

I want to share with you a very personal letter that Billie wrote to me just a few days after becoming aware of my moral failure. God had already done a great work in my heart by bringing me to godly sorrow when I told her about what had happened, and I saw my sin against Him worse than the consequences I would experience as the result of the sin. Because of that, I saw more clearly than ever the magnitude of my sin against my wife, children, friends, and ministry. I knew at that time I could go no further without confessing to Billie Kaye. She wrote this letter only five days after her world came tumbling down around her.

My dear, precious husband,

As I sit here in our daughter's bedroom, my mind seems to swirl with so many thoughts. But it's hard to write everything down the way I want. These are probably the hardest few days I've ever lived through in my 40 years. I faced feelings I've never had to deal with before. I was like King David when he said, "I was brought very low." I read Psalm 130 and memorized it on the plane. "Out of the depths have I cried unto thee, O Lord." He certainly knows how to get us to "cry unto Him." I've never known the full meaning of "depths" before. I know through all of this that Christ will be magnified. God's Word has never been sweeter or the privilege of prayer more comforting. "He who keeps me does not slumber; I know He is my help." So many of the songs I sing have new meaning. I'm grateful for that. The Psalms have also taken on a new meaning. So many times it talks about God being our refuge and strength: He is surely my refuge and strength; my peace and my hiding place.

I believe, as you said tonight when you called, Christ will be glorified through all of this.

I love you very much. I'm grateful to our heavenly Father that you are my husband. I know through this, that God will cause me to be a better help-meet.

Looking unto Jesus,
Billie

I found this letter just a couple of weeks ago in my office as I was going through some keepsakes wrapping up the writing of this book. After more than two decades, I think I wept more when I found it this time than when I first read it.

The reason I want to share it *exactly* as she wrote it is because her attitude and faith in a most difficult situation is what God used to perform a miracle in our marriage. Did she see godly sorrow on my part? Yes. Did she have people around her at that point encouraging her to stay married? *Emphatically no!* But she had a deep and unwavering commitment to Christ, her children, her husband, and her marriage, and God honored that commitment. Our life together now is so far beyond anything we could have asked for or imagined. We are blessed with family, friends, and a future that's nothing short of glorious.

Years ago during our restoration time, we were parked on the ocean in our Prevost bus for a few days of rest. As I started jogging down the beach one morning, I whirled around and started running backward. I saw the footprints I had left in the sand. All of a sudden I started weeping and the Holy Spirit spoke to my heart. It's as if He was saying that we only see God in retrospect. When we're going through a great trial it's as if we can't see God anywhere, but once we've passed through the fire, we can look back and see that He was there—and there—and there, all of the time.

We are running backward through life. Though we don't live in the past, we can look back and see more clearly than ever what the enemy had meant for evil, God turned into good. The enemy said, "I'll ruin them with this," *but God* said, "No you won't. This is what I'll use to make them a vessel fit for the Potter's use." Has it been worth all the tears and sorrow, grief and struggle? Let me say that I regret the wrong choices I made, but not at all what our mighty God has done for us in redeeming us from those choices.

Dear friend, no matter who you are or what your circumstances are, God is a God of miracles. Be willing to face the person in the mirror, let God change your heart, live by faith, and let the song begin. The greatest song ever sung—the song of Amazing Grace.

This is a poem I wrote about Billie in 1977, a few years after we became Christians. Even though I have not always lived what I wrote about her, I have always deeply loved her and believed these words with all of my heart:

A Very Personal Note From Paul

Who can find a virtuous woman
She'll be worth far more than gold
She'll do you good not evil
And love you growing old

That's the way it is with Billie Kaye
The one I love the most
She's sensitive, kind, and generous
A joy to the Heavenly Host

Her love for the Savior thrills me
Her faith when by waves we're tossed
And all because one day by grace
She bowed at the foot of the cross

Her children all adore her
They rise and call her blessed
For she sets them all an example
Of Christian peace and rest

Her friends are many in number
She's loved by every one
Because she loves in word and deed
And not with just her tongue

She is a crown of glory
That anyone can plainly see
And my lips shall ever praise my Lord
For joining her to me

I found a virtuous woman
But can't describe my love
For she has meant the world to me
And shall mean more above

—To my precious wife, Billie Kaye

Reflections

Reflections

_____

_____

_____

_____

_____

_____

_____

_____

_____

Reflections

Reflections

_____

_____

_____

_____

_____

_____

_____

_____

_____

Reflections

Reflections

_____

_____

_____

_____

_____

_____

_____

_____

_____

MINISTRY INFORMATION

*P*aul Tsika is pastor, advisor, and marriage Counselor for World Wide Dream Builders based in Spokane, Washington.

He is the founder of Restoration Ranch, Midfield, Texas, and president of Paul E. Tsika Ministries, Inc. Paul and Billie Kaye reside at Restoration Ranch in Texas where they provide marriage and relationship counseling.

Paul and Billie Kaye's son, Paul Tsika II, earned a Master of Arts in Christian Education with a minor in counseling from Southwestern Seminary in Fort Worth, Texas. He is also the executive director of the Restoration Ranch. Paul II and his wife, Melanie, provide marriage and relationship counseling at the ranch and are available for marriage conferences and retreats.

Office: 361-588-7190

Website: www.plowon.org

Email: paultsika2@yahoo.com

DESTINY IMAGE PUBLISHERS, INC.

*"Speaking to the Purposes of God for This Generation
and for the Generations to Come."*

VISIT OUR NEW SITE HOME AT
WWW.DESTINYIMAGE.COM

FREE SUBSCRIPTION TO DI NEWSLETTER

Receive free unpublished articles by top DI authors, exclusive

discounts, and free downloads from our best and newest books.

Visit www.destinyimage.com to subscribe.

Write to: Destiny Image
              P.O. Box 310
              Shippensburg, PA 17257-0310

Call: 1-800-722-6774

Email: orders@destinyimage.com

For a complete list of our titles or to place an order
online, visit www.destinyimage.com.

FIND US ON FACEBOOK OR FOLLOW US ON TWITTER.

www.facebook.com/destinyimage   **facebook**
www.twitter.com/destinyimage   **twitter**